Christian A. S

Color Your World

with

Natural Church Development

Experiencing all that God has
designed you to be

ChurchSmart
RESOURCES

Color Your World with Natural Church Development is based on the predecessor book *Natural Church Development* that focusses on presenting the findings of the initial research project.

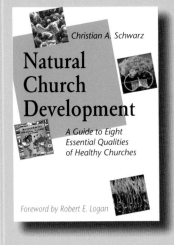

Christian A. Schwarz
Natural Church Development
Hardcover, 128 pages, fully illustrated, with over 100 full-color photos and graphics
ISBN 1-889638-00-5
Retail price $20.00 in U.S. dollars

Working material related to the theory and practice of Natural Church Development is available in about 40 languages. Titles and ordering information can be found on the internet at:
www.ncd-international.org
www.ChurchSmart.com

Registered readers of this book will receive **free access to the web site** www.ncd-international.org/community. There you will find:

- Six *mini-seminars* by the author on each of the six chapters
- *Background information* on the contents of every chapter
- The *graphics* of this book for use in your own presentations

Your **access code** is provided on page 162.

Retail price $20.00 – Quantity discounts available
Call 1-800-253-4276 for current pricing
Published by ChurchSmart Resources, St. Charles, IL 60174
© 2005 by Christian A. Schwarz, NCD Media, Emmelsbüll, Germany
© U.S.A. edition: 2005 by ChurchSmart Resources
3830 Ohio Ave., St. Charles, IL 60174
Edited by Jon & Kathy Haley
Layout and artwork by Christian A. Schwarz
Scripture taken from *Holy Bible: New International Version®*
© 1973, 1978, 1984 by International Bible Society. Used by permission of Zondervan Publishing House. All rights reserved.
Printing: M.C.E. HOREB, Viladecavalls (Barcelona) – Printed in Spain
Photocopying not allowed. All rights reserved.
ISBN 1-889638-47-1

Color Your World with Natural Church Development

Table of contents

Chapter 4: The Minimum Factor

Chapter 5: The Tools

Chapter 6: Your Starting Point

An invitation to join a global movement

Y ou cannot apply for membership to this community, nor can you support it by donations. It's a community that functions without committees and charismatic gurus, that has neither a public relations nor a fund raising department. It's a community whose foundations are exclusively based on biblical principles, research findings, and personal relationships. Doesn't sound like an impressive enterprise so far, does it?

However, this community is mushrooming. Over the past seven years, it has established roots in more than 40,000 churches. To date, 70 countries have decided to launch their own national branches. And millions of Christians have discovered what this community is all about: drawing people closer to the triune God, helping them experience all that God has in store for them and, as a natural side effect, seeing numerical growth within the church as a whole.

The NCD principles are the paint; the NCD tools are the brush. I invite you to pick up the brush and begin painting.

The NCD Community

The name of this community is hardly ever mentioned, and yet there is a name. It's the *NCD Community*. NCD stands for Natural Church Development, the label for an approach to the Christian life—both on an individual and corporate level—that combines fundamental biblical principles with insights that have been brought to light by the most comprehensive church growth research that has ever been done.

NCD is a truly international community; it's neither western nor oriental, neither typical of the northern nor the southern hemisphere of this world. It's an intercultural learning experience. In the same way, the NCD Community is truly interdenominational. It's neither Protestant nor Roman Catholic, neither Baptist nor Pentecostal, neither Lutheran nor Presbyterian, neither mainline nor independent, or we could say: It's all of this, and much more. There are countless Christians representing all of these different denominations who have applied NCD to their own theological and spiritual traditions and have experienced highly encouraging results.

How to join the movement

Right from the outset, I want to make the purpose of this book crystal clear. I would like to persuade you to join this community, if you should sense that you are not already a part of it. How can you join? No application form, no registration, no fees. You join this community simply by sharing its principles. And you share its principles, not by verbal affirmation, but by applying them to your personal life and to the life of your church.

However, I have one warning: Once you have joined this community, it will be difficult for you to leave it, since that would require that you no longer apply the very principles that will have brought a new level of effectiveness to your personal life and to the life of your church. Throughout the course of this book, you will discover why these principles are so powerful: They are not made by humans, but created by God himself.

The principles apply to your personal context, to your sphere of influence, to your world.

My experiences:

Throughout this book, you will see this headline. In these spaces I will share experiences that I have gained in my own ministry, usually as a part of NCD conferences. Outside the context of this book, many of these experiences may seem meaningless, but their purpose here is to illustrate some of the principles that are dealt with in the main text. They will help reinforce the fact that NCD has not been developed in front of a computer screen, but in the midst of personal interactions with Christians of many diverse backgrounds.

What are universal principles?

Over the past few years, I have repeatedly experienced a serious communication problem. The expression "universal principles" is a term that is loaded with positive emotions for me. Numerous encounters with many wonderful Christians on all six continents instantly flash through my memory. The sheer mention of this term brings to mind many of their faces, their stories, and the victories and sorrows that we have shared in so many different settings.

However, when I use this term in my lectures, hardly anyone in the audience shares my enthusiasm. For the majority of them, it is just another abstract term: blood-less, scientific, high and dry. There are no inner pictures, no faces, no stories that come to mind.

Shifting to the Second Chapter

When the original book, *Natural Church Development,* was published in December 1996, it couldn't refer to the NCD Community, since at that time NCD did not yet exist as a global movement. The book could only present our initial research findings in the form of principles.

Now the situation has changed. By God's grace, NCD has advanced from the abstractness of global principles to the vibrant life of a global movement. The consequences are far-reaching: Research findings deal with correlation coefficients; movements deal with people. Research findings present numbers; within a movement we see faces. Research findings verify or falsify theses; in a movement we tell stories. This shift is what we call the *Second Chapter of NCD.*

What's different?

Color Your World with Natural Church Development covers the same basic content as the original book. The most important new features of the book you are holding in your hands are the following:

• It approaches NCD primarily from the individual believer's point of view rather than limiting itself to the pastor's perspective.

• It takes the application of the NCD principles to a personal level, not just to a church or small group level.

Natural Church Development means people meeting, interacting, learning, praying: Leaders from all six continents at the 2004 NCD World Summit in Pretoria, South Africa.

• It places the *Trinitarian Compass*—that has since become a chief tool for implementing NCD—at the center of every chapter.

• It explicitly emphasizes the benefits of an inter-cultural approach that, probably more than any other feature, has become a hallmark of NCD.

In this new book, I want to share with you as much as possible of what I have been privileged to learn over the past nine years. I hope that I can also communicate the overwhelming joy that it has been for me to work alongside so many different Christians within the NCD Community.

Color Your World

I have chosen the title, *Color Your World with Natural Church Development*. The underlying metaphor is that the NCD principles are the paint, the NCD tools (such as this book) are the brush. Now that the paint and the brush are at your disposal, I invite you to discover which colors are most needed, pick up your brush and begin painting.

This book is about painting *your world*. Sure, NCD was originally formulated as the result of a search for universal principles of church growth, but it would be misleading to reduce the applicability of NCD principles to the church. They are equally applicable to the lives of individual believers. They apply to your personal context, to your sphere of influence, to *your* world. And if your sphere of influence is a small group or a denomination or the political life of a whole country, then these are the areas where the NCD principles apply.

After all, what is the church? The church is people. What determines the health of a church? The health of the heads, hands, and hearts of those people. How can we enhance the health of a church? By enhancing the health of our heads, hands, and hearts. The results? Growing churches that fulfill their God-given purpose, that develop their own individuality, that influence and transform society. I would like to see you as a part of that movement.

Together in His service,
Christian A. Schwarz

More on the web:

*Wherever you see this headline, you will find a list of additional questions that are not directly dealt with in this book. By inserting your **access code** (provided on page 162) you can log onto the web page, **www.ncd-international.org/community** to find answers to these questions. You will also find additional information related to the topics of this book.*

At the end of each section, you will find a question for personal reflection inside this yellow box.

Explore the Second Chapter of NCD

1

In its first phase, NCD focused on identifying universal principles of church growth. Some people have missed what this abstract-sounding phrase really means: principles of life that are applicable to Christians in Africa as well as in Asia, in Australia as well as in Europe, in Latin America as well as in North America. They apply regardless of your theological bent, your philosophy of ministry, or your favorite church model. They apply to your personal life as well as to the life of your church. And they apply even if you decide not to utilize them.

Your dream church

If I were sitting next to you now, it wouldn't take long for me to figure out how you feel about the concepts of "church growth" or "church development." Even without putting your feelings into words, I would probably be able to detect them from watching your eyes, observing your gestures, and listening to the sound of your voice. This sort of information would be extremely helpful to me given the topic I want to share with you in this book.

Mixed feelings

If you were to share your feelings with me, what would they be? If you are like most Christians I have met, the term "church development" probably does not bring strong enthusiastic emotions to the surface. It's not unlikely that you share the same skepticism that I frequently encounter with other people when discussing this topic. Many of us have the vague suspicion that when we talk about church development, we are referring to some sort of marketing gimmick or manipulative, pushy method... that our emphasis is on quantity... that we are trying to copy a successful model church... that we are about to import an approach that doesn't really fit our own culture... that we are hoping to implement some successful pastor's pet ideas that have nothing to do with the reality in our own churches.

If these are your feelings, I assure you that I agree with you 100 percent. Those approaches do indeed exist, and my own feelings toward them are not different from yours.

Just imagine...

However, I would like to invite you to perform a brief mental exercise. Imagine that there was an approach to church growth that didn't sport the latest marketing trick, but that was built on a sound **theological foundation** that you could identify with, and that this theological compass permeated even the most practical aspects of church life. Imagine that this approach was not focused on quantity (more people, higher numbers), but that it held **quality** at the center of all considerations.

Imagine an approach to church growth that doesn't copy a model church, but is focused on developing a church's **individuality** and releasing its God-given creativity. Imagine that this approach doesn't export features from one specific culture, but strives to create an **inter-cultural** learning experience, in which all cultures give and take.

Imagine an approach to church growth that doesn't simply promote the favorite ideas of some successful leader, but is

> ## Many of us don't have any mental pictures of what a healthy church looks like.

My experiences:

At the start of NCD conferences, I like to invite the participants to close their eyes and recall a situation in which they have felt completely happy and relaxed. When asking for feedback, usually more than 80 percent indicate that some mental image has come to their mind: a walk on the beach, sitting with friends in a pub, enjoying a candlelight dinner with their spouse. Then I ask them to close their eyes again, and take note of the images that come to mind when they think of a "healthy church." The result? The majority have not been able to come up with any mental pictures related to this concept. Obviously, nothing of this kind has been stored in the memory of most Christians.

Any church, no matter how unfavorable its present situation, can expect considerable increase in quality and quantity. To start such a process, there is only one precondition: a longing for God to manifest himself more strongly in the life of a church.

based on the comprehensive **research** of thousands of churches around the globe. That communicates truly universal **principles**. That helps you fulfill your own dreams for your church. That is fun to be involved in. Wouldn't you be curious to learn more about it?

The core of NCD

The features I have just mentioned are, in fact, the very center of what I have chosen to call Natural Church Development. It is a privilege for me to invite you to join millions of other believers from 70 countries who have already begun this journey and are experiencing highly promising results.

Working with so many churches in so many different settings, I have learned that there is no precondition either you or your church has to fulfill in order to commence this journey. Whether you are a mature believer or still unexperienced in your Christian faith; whether you have adopted an orthodox theology or find yourself on the other end of the theological spectrum; whether you are a member of a quickly growing church or a congregation that has been in decline for decades; whether you are an advocate of one of the famous model churches or you are hesitant to jump on their bandwagon—the principles outlined in this book will help you experience greater effectiveness both in your personal life and in the life of your church.

Are there truly no preconditions to getting started? Actually, there is *one*. There must be a longing in your heart to experience more of what God has in store for you and your church. If you don't have this longing, this book will not speak to you. However, if you do, you have all you need to begin a journey that could well become one of the most adventurous undertakings of your life. Let's link arms and travel together.

What would your ideal of a healthy church look like? Which details would be important for you?

Startling results from 70 countries

Chapter 1

A s of the writing of this book, 40,000 churches have participated—with differing levels of intensity—in the NCD process. Since all of them have conducted at least one NCD Survey (which means that 30 members have completed a detailed questionnaire) we have the data of most of these churches in our computers and are able to monitor their actual results, both in terms of quality and quantity.

51% increase of the growth rate

Recently we selected all of the churches that have done three NCD Surveys and compared their initial numbers (at the time of their first survey) with their most recent results (at the time of their third survey, which was completed, on average, 31 months later). At the time of the third survey, the quality of these churches had increased by an average of 6 points. Later in this book, I will explain what these points mean. For the time being, it's enough to know that they indicate considerably more love, more forgiveness, more answers to prayer, more wisdom, more spiritual power, and countless other quality factors in those churches. Great.

But what about the quantity? Did the focus on church quality actually result in numerical growth, as NCD claims it does? Here are the results. By the time of the third survey the average growth rate of all participating churches had increased by 51%. If a church had been growing at a rate of 10 people per year before beginning the process, 31 months into the process, that number had grown to 15 people per year; if there had been 200 people per year joining the church previously, now there were 302. In addition, due to the NCD process, the percentage of transfer growth decreased, while the percentage of conversion growth increased. These results are illustrated in the diagram on page 13. The upper part of the right bar symbolizes the additional growth experienced due to the NCD process.

How many people?

If you study the diagram, the whole topic might still appear rather abstract. However, you shouldn't forget that the bars of this diagram represent individual people—most of them who didn't know Christ previously and came into a personal relationship with him. According to our calculations, we can assume that by now approximately 1.3 million individuals have joined these churches as a direct consequence of the NCD process. A closer look at these 1.3 million people reveals that they are very special people, as the following three criteria apply to all of them.

1. The number 1.3 million is not the overall growth of the churches that have invested themselves in the NCD process (that number is considerably higher), but just the *additional* growth that occurred after they started to apply NCD principles consciously.

After eight years of NCD, we can see a breakthrough in terms of people joining the church.

My experiences:

For me personally, it's an exhilarating experience to learn from the data we have collected, since they show us how church development actually functions in real life, regardless of our own theories. As the data of all surveyed churches contain 168 million individual responses and encompass an enormous variety of different cultures, denominations, and theological persuasions, it enables our team to base our conclusions on a solid foundation.

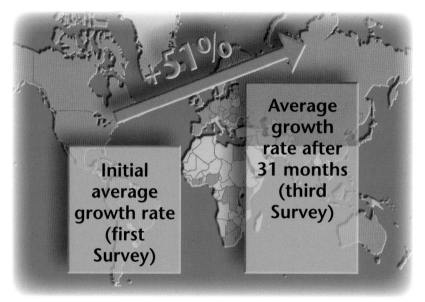

Initial average growth rate (first Survey)

Average growth rate after 31 months (third Survey)

+51%

The average growth rate of all of the churches that did a third NCD Survey, increased by 51%. At the time of this writing (June 2005) this has resulted in 1.3 million additional people who have joined the participating churches as a consequence of applying NCD principles.

2. As the quality of these churches grew substantially over the same time frame, these new members are members of "high quality" churches. As everyone who has experienced first-hand the effects of the qualitative approach can affirm, members of higher quality churches live very different lives than members of lower quality churches.

3. All of these 1.3 million people are incorporated in a local church. According to all serious studies on evangelistic outreach that I have seen so far, it's realistic to assume that only between 15% (in the best-case scenario) and 0.3% (in the worst-case scenario) of people who give their lives to Christ in the context of an evangelistic campaign will be members of a local church one year later. In NCD we only count those people who are involved in a local church. Just for the sake of comparison: In order to win 1.3 million people applying "classic procedures," we would have to get "decisions" of between 8.5 million people (in the best case) and 433 million people (in the worst case).

More on the web:

On the internet (see page 162) you will find answers to the following questions:

• *How much of NCD growth is conversion growth, how much is simply transfer growth?*

• *How has the 51% increase been measured?*

What the figures stand for

Figures, figures, figures. Perhaps I should stop here. Much more interesting than the figures themselves is studying how they came about. The quantitative growth was a natural side effect of these churches' attempts to grow in quality. This growth in quality has released an almost magnetic attraction, enabling them to experience what Paul teaches us in 1 Corinthians 3:6: We plant, we water. But God gives the increase.

What strategy does your church follow to win people to Christ? What have the results been so far?

The NCD Story

The story of Natural Church Development is a story of God's grace. We who are publicly regarded as the founders of NCD, have often felt more like spectators of what God was doing before our very eyes than active players.

The story of NCD is a story of God's grace in action.

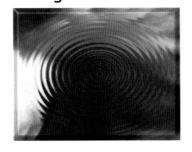

My experiences:

I have heard many speakers say that, when doing a conference, they were the ones that learned the most. In some cases, that might simply be a way to please the audience. However, when I make this statement, it has nothing to do with politeness. Encounters with people in the context of NCD activities have been my number one source of learning. In the past few years, I have had the privilege of doing conferences in 42 countries. How did I gain the insights that I am sharing in this book? First and foremost, by meeting people and interacting with them in the context of my travels.

How it started

When I recall the time of our first international research project, in which 1000 churches from 32 countries participated, I remember that few people believed that what we were setting out to do would have any spiritual or strategic impact. Mild skepticism was the usual response I encountered when telling fellow Christians about the project.

However, I was not willing to accept the fact that after 2000 years of church history and the publication of hundreds of books on church growth, no research had been done at an international level to verify whether or not the "principles" promoted in these books were really universally valid.

Initial results

Actually, this bleak beginning was not that long ago, but for me it seems as if decades have passed since then. When we published our findings at the end of 1996, things literally changed overnight. Many Christians sensed that NCD was not another model, but was really based on universal principles. They began to view it not as a "Western" contribution, but as an opportunity for inter-cultural learning. Within a few years, 70 countries had made the decision to establish their own NCD ministries.

The network approach

We decided to build the NCD infrastructure as a pure network. No committees, no hierarchies, no constitutions. My office is located in what used to be a farm at the Danish border, on top of what used to be the barn. Whenever visitors come to see our "international headquarters," I am proud to show them all that I have there: a desk, a computer, a telephone, many Bibles, electricity, a bed for guests, a wonderful family, and a big and yet unfulfilled vision. I am aware that most of our visitors are disappointed by this "meager infrastructure," since they are expecting a several-story building, numerous secretaries, and a boss sitting in his prestigious office behind an oversized oak-tree desk...

Why am I proud of the infrastructure we have? Because I am absolutely convinced—and there is not a bit of irony involved in it—that it is more modern, more professional, and more effective than many of the "oak-tree approaches" that are so widespread in today's world. We feel per-

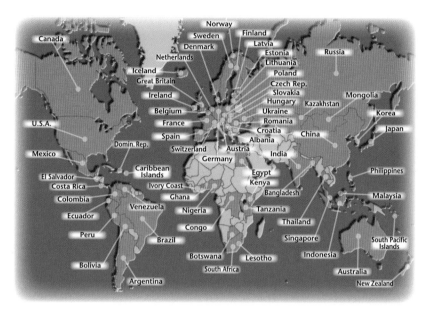

A national NCD ministry already exists or is in preparation in all of the countries highlighted in green on this map. The other countries (orange) do not have an NCD ministry as of the time of this writing. Updated information is provided at www. ncd-international. org.

fectly equipped for the ministry God has called us to do. Why? Because our real infrastructure is people.

A story of people

The true NCD story is a story of people. People like my friend and colleague Christoph Schalk, a trained psychologist and organizational scientist, who made the commitment to invest the rest of his life and all of his expertise into the development of the NCD network.

Or people like Paul Jeong who had the courage to confront many Korean church leaders with a very different approach to church growth than what they had previously encountered, and has built a booming NCD ministry in Korea.

Or people like Ian Campbell and Adam Johnstone from Australia who, from the very beginning, demonstrated an aversion to simply borrowing others' instruments, working to develop many innovative NCD tools that have not only blessed Australia, but churches in many other countries as well.

Or people like Juan Galdamez from El Salvador who switched from teaching at the university to assisting NCD National Partners as the NCD coordinator for Latin America.

Or people like Henrik Andersen who helped launch a two-year NCD process in Denmark with official representatives of almost every Danish denomination, each of whom observed significant qualitative growth in the churches under their care. Even before this process came to an end, Henrik moved to Latvia, where similar developments have since taken place.

More on the web:

On the internet (see page 162) you will find answers to the following questions:

- *What is the relationship of NCD to the church growth movement?*

- *What came first: the theory or the research?*

Or people like Dave Wetzler from the United States whose NCD ministry, like most of ours, started out quite small, but through winning the confidence of countless denominational leaders, has gradually built up the largest national NCD ministry on this planet, with several thousand coaches.

Or people like Medhat Aziz from Egypt whose initiative and sacrificial commitment has made NCD available to churches in the Arab world.

Or people like Silvia Handoko from Indonesia who is at the hub of a revival of New Testament proportions, helping churches to consistently apply NCD principles in the midst of it. She has much to share with the rest of the world about how a *real* revival, as opposed to a widespread—especially Western—revival stereotype, functions in our day and age.

To what extent does each of the values below describe your own value system?

The real story will be written in the future

However, I don't like to tell the NCD story as a story of things of the past. It is the story of the church of the future. It is a story that will be written by those who put Natural Church Development into practice. Only God knows the main actors of that future story. It could well be, however, that he has already decided to make you one of them.

Core values of NCD International

At NCD International, we try to model the same principles that we teach at the local church level. We are convinced that by reflecting the values we believe in we will make a more sustainable impact than by just speaking about them in public conferences. Here are the core values of NCD that permeate all aspects of our ministry:

• **Creativity:** We believe that God has entrusted all human beings with creativity that enables them to find their own solutions and develop their own styles.

• **Diversity:** We generally view a variety of different approaches (cultures, denominations, methods) as being superior to a uniform pattern.

• **Quality:** We regard the quality of ministry as the strategic root for quantitative fruit. All of our activities are focused on increasing the quality of the Christian life.

• **Process:** We are convinced that the key to success is an ongoing, long-term process, and that even the smallest step in the right direction is real progress.

• **Balance:** At all levels of church life, we strive to achieve a biblical balance between the different ministry foci that God wants to see in his church.

• **Focus:** Given the many things that have to be done, we always try to focus on the one specific aspect that has the potential to bring about the greatest progress.

"I have done NCD"

A t NCD conferences when people want to initiate a conversation with me, they frequently say, "I have done NCD." Whenever I hear this phrase, I can be pretty sure that the three letters they are using don't refer to Natural Church Development but to one specific tool that we provide, namely, the NCD Survey.

People who use this phrase definitely don't want to communicate that they have adopted the NCD paradigm or implemented the principles of NCD, but that they have used our main diagnostic tool. Obviously this tool is, in their eyes, so closely connected to what NCD is all about, that the two terms have become synonymous for them.

NCD is not a toolkit

Please don't misunderstand me. I highly recommend the use of the NCD Survey, since this is an eye-opening tool. I want to warn you, however, not to confuse doing the survey with implementing NCD. Doing the survey can be compared to using a thermometer. It can reveal how healthy or sick you are. But just as using a thermometer does not contribute to a healthy lifestyle, doing the NCD Survey alone does not have much to do with applying the NCD principles.

Many people misunderstand NCD as a toolkit and don't recognize that it is a system. A toolkit is a collection of separate instruments that are in no way interrelated. You simply pick out the tool that you need in a given situation to perform a certain task. Without question, it is possible to use the tools that NCD provides in this manner. However, by doing so you will never experience what Natural Church Development is really all about: Church members moving closer to the living God, beginning to reflect the different facets of God's light, attracting more and more people who have not yet met Christ, and sensing that this quantitative growth has virtually happened all by itself.

Dynamics of a healthy lifestyle

Let's assume you use your thermometer regularly, but do not apply any principles of a healthy lifestyle (for instance, a balanced diet or regular exercise), you should not expect that using the thermometer, even if it is a useful tool, will have *any* positive bearing on your health. The same applies to using the NCD Survey, and it also applies to all of the other tools that NCD offers.

Of course, it's natural that most people encounter NCD by discovering a specific component of the system—a certain book, one of the NCD

Loving your neighbor is a typical NCD activity; pressing the keys of a computer keyboard is not.

My experiences:

People who confuse the NCD Survey with the essence of Natural Church Development, tend to see a close affinity between NCD and the world of computers (since the survey depends on computer technology). However, NCD, as such, has nothing at all to do with the world of computers. Encountering God in prayer (NCD quality characteristic 3) or loving both your neighbors and your enemies (NCD quality characteristic 8) or sharing the gospel with others (NCD quality characteristic 7) are very typical NCD activities. Pressing the keys of a computer keyboard is not.

The 5 Basic Components of NCD

8 Quality Characteristics	6 Growth Forces	Trinitarian Compass	Minimum Factor	NCD Tools
The "muscles" of NCD	*The "blood" of NCD*	*The "heart" of NCD*	*The "eyes" of NCD*	*The "hands" of NCD*
The most visible part of the body. At first glance you can see whether or not the muscles are trained. Some muscles may be better trained than others.	Every muscle depends on the circulation of the blood in order to develop. Blood contains the nutrients that the muscles need.	The function of the heart is to pump the blood to the muscles. A heart that stops beating causes the whole organism to die.	Our eyes enable us to focus on specific details. The eyes never see all of reality, just what they deliberately focus on.	Helpful, but not absolutely essential. If necessary, an organism can survive without hands, but definitely not without a heart.
Pages 104-123	**Pages 80-103**	**Pages 44-79**	**Pages 124-145**	**Pages 146-165**

In this table, the five basic components that make up NCD are compared with five different parts of the human body.

principles, the NCD Survey, etc. They may even experience the usefulness of that component in a given situation. In many cases, this kind of introduction to NCD has become the beginning of a long-term process of moving deeper and deeper into the NCD paradigm. However, if this does not happen, you cannot expect to achieve the fruit that is the natural outcome of the NCD paradigm as a whole.

In the table at the top of this page, I have summarized the five basic components of NCD and indicated how they are interrelated. If some of the terms mentioned in this table mean nothing to you at this time, don't worry. This book will introduce you to all of these components step by step. At the end of the book you will have a firm understanding of each of these concepts and will know how to use them in your own context.

Don't confuse principles with tools

Which of the five components of NCD (see table above) are you already familiar with?

But before we dive any deeper into the world of Natural Church Development, I want to make sure that there is no misunderstanding. Applying what we call the *NCD principles* is absolutely essential for every believer; there is actually not even a real choice, since the Bible itself clearly leads us to these principles. Utilizing the *NCD tools,* however, as useful as they might be, doesn't fit in this category. You can do without any of the NCD tools, but you cannot do without the NCD principles. If you don't like the tools, please simply ignore them. But never ignore the principles that these tools seek to communicate.

What is your favorite growth pattern?

It is difficult to appreciate what NCD is all about without fully understanding what we mean by a "principle-oriented approach" to church development. Because different groups associate different meanings with this concept, let me clarify what we mean by it in Natural Church Development.

A principle-oriented approach is based on the assumption that every church has its God-given individuality.

Four criteria of a principle-oriented approach

A principle-oriented approach to church development fulfills the following four criteria:

1. Principles are **universally valid**. They don't apply only to certain situations or specific circumstances. They apply to all denominations, to all church models, to all devotional styles, and to all cultures.

2. Principles must be **proven**. Until we have clear empirical proof, we may be dealing with an interesting concept that is worth consideration, but we shouldn't speak about a principle. There is only one way to find out whether or not a specific feature is a universal principle: research on a universal (i.e. worldwide) scale.

3. Principles always deal with what is **essential**, never with secondary aspects of the Christian life. Therefore, we can expect to find the principles that influence our lives also described in the Bible, even if the terminology is different.

4. Principles always have to be **individualized**. They never tell you exactly what to do. Rather, they give you criteria that enable you to discover what should be done in a given situation.

Not all contributions to church growth are based on a principle-oriented approach. Over the past few years, I have encountered four different patterns that, in some ways, overlap with a principle-oriented approach. I call them the faithfulness pattern, the breakthrough pattern, the model pattern, and the management pattern.

The faithfulness pattern

The faithfulness pattern focuses on a very important aspect of the Christian life. Advocates of this approach rightly stress that we must be faithful, for instance, to the Word of God and to the gifts God has entrusted us with. "No matter how 'successful' a certain method may be, if it's not in line with Scripture, we are not interested." NCD holds this same position.

But representatives of the faithfulness pattern go one step further. They tend to reduce *everything* to faithfulness. When it comes to church development, their motto is, "All we have to do is adopt a specific theology, moral code, form of worship service, political position, etc." According to this view, church health is determined by simply sticking to what a specific group defines as the core of faithfulness. The most radical adherents to this approach do not even deem it necessary for a church to grow.

The breakthrough pattern

> **Many Christians are waiting for a breakthrough, but are unaware of the dynamics that make such a breakthrough likely to happen.**

The second pattern, which I call the breakthrough pattern, is especially widespread among charismatic groups, but not limited to them. In most cases, the awaited breakthrough is a revival. Since revivals are God-given and advance the kingdom tremendously, all of us should be praying for revival and do our best to prepare our churches for it. That is what we are committed to do in NCD.

But once again, representatives of the breakthrough pattern tend to take it one step further. Many of them diminish the relevance of the down-to-earth activities that are the very foundation upon which a revival can flourish (for instance, working on all of the quality characteristics of a healthy church). Some groups hold the assumption that if you attend a specific conference, are baptized in the Spirit, follow a certain leader, or apply a successful prayer technique, you will bring about a breakthrough in your church. The desire for a spiritual breakthrough is often pitted against long-term, process-driven, principle-oriented contributions to church development.

The model pattern

A third widespread pattern of church growth is the model pattern. Generally, a model-oriented approach can be very powerful. Model churches enable you to encounter the principles of church development by dealing with concrete case studies. There is much to be learned from church models. In fact, everything that I have learned about church development stems from concrete models, they may encompass 30 or 3000 people, they may be found in the Western world or in Asia, Africa, or Latin America. What else should model churches be than churches that display extraordinarily high quality? Studying these kinds of churches is exactly what we do in NCD research.

Representatives of the model pattern, however, go a step further. Rather than dealing with many different models they focus on one single church model. Even when they talk about principles ("Don't imitate the model, but follow the principles!"), they usually mean something different than what we mean by this concept in NCD. They are referring to the principles *behind their specific model* rather than the principles that apply to any church model in any culture.

The management pattern

The management pattern seeks to transfer insights from the business world to the sphere of the church. Since a lot of business techniques are nothing other than social sciences

My experiences:

Ten years ago the distinction between a principle and a model-oriented approach was not even an established category. This has radically changed, and I attribute it, at least in part, to our contributions to the discussion on church development. At the beginning of the NCD ministry, I often heard that people had difficulty with the fact that I am not a local pastor (a typical concern that arises from a model-driven mentality, where the expectation was that I would promote the model of my home church). In the past five years, however, I haven't heard this criticism one single time. I take this as another sign that people are beginning to grasp what a principle-oriented approach is all about.

Five church growth patterns or only two?

1. Faithfulness
2. Breakthrough
3. Model
4. Management

5. Principles

This table summarizes the five church growth patterns mentioned in this chapter. It also reveals that we are not really speaking of five different categories, but only two (A and B).

applied to specific organizations, this is a legitimate approach. Many Christians would be well advised to learn from the business world.

But representatives of the management pattern tend to reduce church development completely to business techniques. They may still refer to the Holy Spirit, but for all practical purposes he is no longer needed. Business techniques have taken his place. In these groups people fail to see that not every management method is applicable in the church. Many of these techniques are not as "neutral" as it is often assumed. Rather, they are based on a distinct concept of humanity that sometimes contradicts the biblical concept.

The principle-oriented approach

Look at the diagram at top of this page. I have placed the four patterns that I have just discussed in box A, and the principle-oriented approach in box B. This diagram communicates that we are not actually dealing with five different patterns, but that the decisive distinction is between paradigm A (patterns 1-4) and paradigm B (pattern 5). The principle-oriented approach seeks to integrate the truths behind each of the four patterns mentioned above, while avoiding their one-sided views.

It is helpful to take a look at different movements and ask yourself which of the five approaches they reflect. Take, for instance, a widespread Lutheran view (you will find similar patterns in other denominations as well): "Our only contribution to church development is proclaiming the Word and administering the sacraments." What kind of pattern does this reflect? You have probably guessed correctly: the faithfulness pattern. Or, which pattern is most widespread in the charismatic movement? It's the breakthrough pattern, sometimes mixed with elements of other patterns.

To make things more concrete, let's take a look at a famous model church, Willow Creek. For those of you who haven't heard of it, Willow Creek is an evangelical church in the United States, planted by Bill Hybels and famous for its seeker-sensitive worship services. Countless church leaders around the globe have been inspired by the ministry of Willow Creek and have sought to build similar churches in their own contexts.

Where does Willow Creek fit in?

> NCD seeks to integrate the truths behind each of the different patterns, while avoiding their one-sided views.

Which of the five patterns is at the root of Willow Creek? Be careful, the answer is not as obvious as it might appear at first sight. When I ask this question in conferences, the first reaction is usually to put Willow Creek into the "model" category. However, you should take a closer look at the original Willow Creek Church in South Barrington, Illinois. Is it a model-oriented church? In no way. Bill Hybels doesn't follow another church model, but clearly seeks God's calling for himself and his church. Willow Creek has become so successful because they have applied universal principles to the challenges of their specific cultural context. In other words, Bill Hybels has followed paradigm B.

Many of the churches that try to imitate Willow Creek today, however, have actually adopted the model pattern and are following paradigm A. They are in danger of missing the very secret that has made Willow Creek so successful: applying a "paradigm B approach." Do you really want to learn from Willow Creek? Then learn that they never imitated the model of another church.

Models and principles

Let's assume you are following a certain church model. Do I want to convince you to give that up? By no means. Rather, my desire is to draw your attention to *why* some model churches have become successful: Consciously or unconsciously they have applied the universal principles of church development. That's the secret of their success.

More on the web:

On the internet (see page 162) you will find answers to the following questions:

- *Is there any church model that, from an NCD point of view, is superior to others?*

- *Is it better to apply NCD principles with or without the help of a specific church model?*

You can look at extremely different models. Compare for instance, Willow Creek and the house church movement. One model is focused on a megachurch; the other teaches that no church should have more than 20 members. One model prides itself in spectacular buildings; in the other, no church buildings are allowed. One model is characterized by a large staff; the other, as a matter of principle, has no full-time workers. One model has a high view of professionalism; in the other, professionalism is almost regarded as a sin.

> Which of the five patterns mentioned in this chapter has influenced you the most?

These are huge differences indeed. What do these two models have in common? And what do they share with countless other wonderful church models? Nothing other than the principles that we have chosen to call Natural Church Development.

Natural Church Development and spiritual unity

Chapter 1

Every church model that I have dealt with communicates *both* universal principles of church development *and* the specifics of that very model. The problem is, however, that the leaders of the model churches usually don't make a clear distinction between these two categories. They are so convinced of the significance of their models' distinctives that they tend to endorse them as principles, which can be quite confusing.

NCD focuses on the elements that different Christian groups have in common.

Why the distinction is important

In every church, whether it is regarded as a model or not, you can identify both categories: the application of universal principles and additional elements. These additional elements make up the identity of a church and create the differences between individual churches and church movements.

I am convinced that this is a positive thing. Since Christian churches are so different, they are able to win many outsiders with differing backgrounds, tastes, interests, and styles. I definitely don't want to argue against the distinctives of church models. In most cases, they are a blessing to the body of Christ. But I want to argue strongly against confusing these distinctives with "principles."

Is it really that important to make this distinction? Yes, it is, at least when it comes to the question of Christian unity. One of the blessings of many church models is that they have managed to bring together believers from the most diverse denominational backgrounds. Thus you get the impression that there is a strong unity-building power behind the model-oriented approach, and to a certain degree, this observation is correct. However, a closer look reveals that this kind of unity depends on saying "Yes" to the distinctives of that specific model. If you disagree with those distinctives, you are no longer united.

Focus on what we have in common

In NCD, we are aware of the distinctives of different movements and we appreciate them. But we don't teach them. We deliberately try to focus on the elements that different Christian groups have in common. Because of that, you really cannot be "against" Natural Church Development, since that would imply being against the very principles that all healthy churches share, consciously or unconsciously. Consider the following three areas:

1. The **principles** that we identified in our research are manifested in all healthy churches. Take a look, for example, at the quality characteristic that we call "passionate spirituality." This characteristic does not imply a specific style. Pentecostals, for

My experiences:

Whenever someone argues that he or she is "against NCD," I deliberately respond in this way: "OK, let's take a look at the individual NCD principles. One of them is loving relationships. If you are against it, you probably are in favor of hatred in your church. I have a number of ideas how to cultivate hatred that I would love to share with you. Another principle is passionate spirituality. If you are against it, you might be interested in boring spirituality. I can assure you that, as a German, I am very experienced in boring spirituality. I would be delighted to help you put it into practice." In a similar way, I go through all of the NCD principles. After a while, everyone agrees that you really cannot take a general position against NCD.

instance, apply this principle very differently than Presbyterians. But the principle is the same. You will learn more about how this works in chapter 3, where we exclusively deal with the principles of NCD.

> ## The goal and criteria of ecumenical encounters is to become demonstrably more effective in ministry.

2. The same holds true for the theological heart of NCD, the **Trinitarian Compass** (chapter 2). This compass enables creative learning exchanges between the most diverse Christian groups. No group has to hide its identity; every one has something to give and to receive. The compass enables a type of ecumenical encounter that is light-years away from an ecumenicism that focuses on committees and papers. The goal and criteria of ecumenical encounters is to become demonstrably more effective in ministry.

3. A third area is the **inter-cultural** approach. As we will see later (pages 28-32), NCD tries to integrate insights from the different cultural poles that make up today's world. A short look at the daily news should convince each of us that tackling this question is no luxury, but one of the most needed tasks of our time.

An undiscovered potential

I am convinced that the unity-building power inherent in the principle-oriented approach is one of the secrets of NCD that still waits to be discovered by countless Christian groups. But even today, these processes have already started at local and regional levels.

More on the web:

On the internet (see page 162) you will find answers to the following questions:

- *What kind of denominations are involved with NCD?*
- *What is the theological basis of NCD International?*

In many countries, there are support groups for NCD in which pastors and lay leaders from different denominations gather together. Though these leaders, when discussing their theological or practical particularities, might normally be in conflict with one another, in these networks, the Roman Catholic priest helps the Baptist pastor become more effective in loving relationships, and in turn the Baptist helps the Catholic think more creatively about evangelism; the charismatics learn from the liberals about empowering leadership, and the liberals experience passionate spirituality in a fresh way as they interact with charismatics. These things are experienced by thousands of Christians on a daily basis in most of the countries that have joined the NCD network; and they take place at NCD conferences as well.

What have been your experiences with ecumenical encounters? Have they been more positive or negative?

Redefining ecumenicism

Recently, a pastor told me, "Christian, you may not be aware of this, but I regard NCD as a serious alternative to the ecumenical movement." I replied, "Thank you for your strong words, but I disagree with you. It is not an alternative to the ecumenical movement. It *is* an ecumenical movement."

The quality approach—often criticized, seldom understood

In Natural Church Development, we don't ask the question, "How do we get more people to attend church?" Nor do we set goals for the numerical size of the church, such as, "By the end of 2008 we will have 2,600 people." What we *do*, however, is focus on the quality of the church. In *this* area, we set precise goals and are eager to reach those goals. We want to see our churches grow in quality and we want to experience the effects of that quality.

One of these effects, as is clearly documented by our research in 40,000 churches, is that churches that improve in quality grow in quantity as well. If we were to summarize the net result of our discoveries in one sentence, it would be this: Quantity is not a strategic goal, but a natural consequence of a healthy church. If a church is healthy—documented by a measurably high quality—quantitative growth will happen "all by itself."

Why it is important to measure quality

In our institute, we have invested many years into developing a scientific instrument to measure the quality of a church— a "thermometer" of church health, so to speak. Since this tool is now available in every country where an NCD National Partner exists (see map on page 15), it enables every church that is interested to get the following pieces of information:

1. What is the overall quality of our church?

2. At this moment, what should be our strategic emphasis in terms of church health (we call this the "minimum factor")?

3. After having worked on that area for a year: How much progress did our church make in qualitative growth?

As long as no tool was available to measure church quality (which was the case until 1996), "church quality" was the foggiest term on planet earth. Though almost everyone was in favor of church quality, there was no way to truly identify whether a church displayed high quality or not. And, ironically, the term was used as an excuse among declining churches: "We are more interested in quality than in quantity."

The situation has changed

Therefore, I do understand why representatives of the church growth movement have attacked this comfortable, but foggy, notion of emphasizing church quality (which couldn't be measured anyway) instead of striving for a higher quantity (which could be easily measured).

In NCD, quality is the root; quantity, the natural fruit.

My experiences:

I have repeatedly heard, especially by people trained in church growth methods, that NCD teaches churches not to set goals. Of course, we do teach goal-setting, but not in the area of quantity ("How many people do we intend to win by a given date?"). Rather, we encourage goal-setting in the area of quality ("What level of health do we want to achieve in the next twelve months?"). In fact, constant goal-setting and a consistent evaluation of the degree to which goals have been met, is a major feature of the NCD cycle. How, then, could the rumor spread that we are opposed to goal setting? The answer is simple: If only quantitative goals count as "true goals," then the NCD procedure has little in common with goal-setting.

> ## The quality of a church is the quality of its people— and nothing more.

What many people—both within the church growth movement and among its critics—have not noticed, however, is that this situation has drastically changed since 1996, with the introduction of the NCD Survey. Since it has become possible to measure quality precisely, the term quality has lost all of its foggy character. Now we can speak about church quality in very precise terms. We can see whether or not we have reached our qualitative goals. And we can study how our focus on quality actually contributes to the quantitative growth of the church.

Quality as a manageable term

This shift has far-reaching consequences. Since church quality has become something measurable, it has enabled us to use qualitative categories in strategic planning. Does your own church have a high, a medium, or a low quality? Ten years ago, you could only guess. If you had asked three people, you might have received three different responses. Now it's possible to get a very precise answer to this question.

Is it possible that your church displays a very high quality in some areas, whereas in others, the quality is quite low? The NCD Survey will bring those realities to light. Is it possible that, after focusing on a specific area, you are not sure whether you have made any progress? The NCD Survey will give you just this piece of information.

Misconceptions about quality

Since the term "church quality" had for so long been an extremely foggy term that everyone defined according to his or her own interest, there are still a number of misconceptions connected to it. By explaining what this term does *not* mean in Natural Church Development, I hope to provide a more solid understanding of how we use this term in our work:

• In NCD, quality is *not* a synonym for **excellence**. Excellence implies setting a very high standard as the goal for everybody. From an NCD point of view, I regard the fashionable preoccupation with excellence more critically than positively. These standards of excellence, which are frequently imported from highly professional megachurches, usually result in setting unrealistic (and thus frustrating) standards for average Christians, rather than helping them release the full potential that God has implanted in *them*.

• Quality is *not* **static**. Far more important than the actual level of quality that your church has attained is whether or not there has been progress over the past few months. If you move from "incredibly bad"

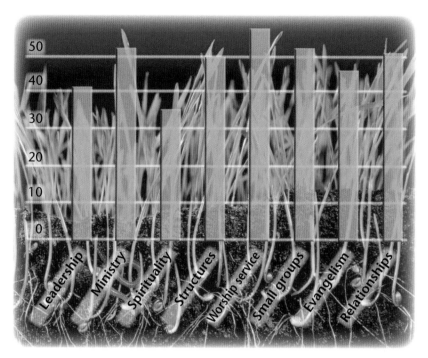

This is an example of the NCD Survey, taken from a church in Brazil. The profile reveals the quality of the church in eight essential areas. This tool enables the church to speak about quality in precise terms and to place quality growth at the center of strategic planning. More specific information on the NCD Survey is provided on page 152.

to "bad" and from there to "not so bad," that is real progress that should be celebrated. If John or Judy are involved in evangelism, their standard for comparison should not be Billy Graham, but John's or Judy's capacity to evangelize one year ago. If it has increased, they have reason to thank God.

• Quality should *not* be confused with **professionalism**. A great show on the platform that responds to a consumer mentality in the pews might be seen as an expression of high professionalism, but in NCD terms it would count as poor quality. What we measure in the NCD Survey is the actual life of the people in the pews, not how well they have been entertained.

• Quality does *not* refer to buildings, toilets, sound-systems or any other **equipment**, but to the quality that is found in the heads, hands and hearts of the people who make up the church.

This is likely the most challenging point for each of us. The quality of your church really has little to do with the height of the church steeple or the salary of your pastor or the age of the organ. But it has a lot to do with... you. Of course, you as an individual are only one part of your church. But I promise you that as you grow in quality as an individual believer, and encourage your friends at church to grow together with you, there will be visible repercussions throughout your whole church body. Qualitative growth is contagious—it multiplies all by itself.

More on the web:

On the internet (see page 162) you will find answers to the following questions:

• What standard is used to decide which aspects are "qualitative factors," and which ones are not?

• Can churches with a low quality expect to grow?

At this moment, would you regard your home church as a "high quality church"? Why or why not?

Chapter 1

Why we need to learn from other cultures

Throughout this book, you will encounter the inter-cultural character of the NCD paradigm. Within our network of NCD National Partners, we distinguish three cultural poles: the West, the East, and the South (see diagram on page 29).

Of course, the diversity within these cultural zones is as abundant as it is between them, since each of them encompasses many diverse languages, customs, histories, and thought patterns. Nevertheless, each cultural zone has characteristic tendencies. This doesn't mean that every individual within each zone displays those characteristics, but it does mean that the percentage of individuals within a given zone who display those characteristics is higher than in the other zones. It's extremely beneficial to take a closer look at each of the three cultural poles.

> ## The very aspects lacking in one culture are provided by another.

My experiences:

We frequently receive letters and e-mails directed to the German NCD Partner, and he receives messages directed to us. Obviously, many people assume that since the offices of NCD International are located in Germany, we are the German NCD Partner. However, that is not the case. We have exactly the same relationship to the German NCD Partner as we have to the Egyptian or American or Indonesian partners. We are well aware that most ministry organizations function differently. They treat their international ministries as branches of their national organization and place the international work under the authority of their national leaders. There are good reasons why we decided to follow a different pattern in NCD.

The Western pole: Competition

The Western pole encompasses both North America and Europe. (Though Australia is culturally related to the Western world as well, due to its geographical positioning, on the very border between the Eastern and the Southern poles, it has an identity of its own.) When studying Western cultures you will usually find a high view of the individual, of self-realization, and of diversity. Values such as freedom of the individual and personal initiative play a more critical role in the Western world than they do in other cultures.

When the two values of freedom and diversity are combined, their synthesis is "competition." While there is competition in other cultures as well, in no other is it viewed as positively as in the West. Whether you look at the economic, the educational, the political, or even the church system, in the Western world you will detect a competitive spirit everywhere.

The prevailing thought pattern in the Western world is linear: cause and effect, input-output, A to B to C. There are many things that can be wonderfully explained by applying linear thinking; but the Western tendency is to apply this thought pattern even when it doesn't fit.

Danger: Domination

There are strengths in the Western paradigm, and there are weaknesses. One of the most obvious dangers may be the tendency toward "navel-gazing." However, the greatest danger of Western cultures is probably their inherent tendency to dominate others. Is imperialism typical of the Western world? Of course it is. This doesn't imply that every Westerner is, by definition, an imperialist. But even those of us who try to resist imperialistic tendencies have to admit that

In today's world, we can distinguish three cultural poles: the West, the East, and the South. Each of these poles displays specific characteristics that would be beneficial for the other poles to learn from.

an imperialistic mind-set has shaped the Western culture as a whole. These tendencies can even be detected in many well-intentioned Christian initiatives.

The Eastern pole: Harmony

The Eastern world, which encompasses most of Asia, functions very differently. Traditionally, these cultures are built on consensus rather than competition. The necessities of rice communities—a form of agriculture that depends to a high degree on the co-operation of the whole village—have shaped many Asian countries. For example, the role of the traditional Indonesian village elder is not to dictate decisions (as it might appear from the outside to Westerners), but to lead the *musyawarah* in a way that encourages dialogue and leads to consensus. That's definitely different than the way the Greek *polis,* which provided the model for Western democracy, used to function.

The different expressions that Asian languages use for peace—such as *wa* in Japanese, *guanxi* in Chinese, or *inhwa* in Korean—are not only different words, but quite different concepts. What they have in common, however, is an extraordinarily high view of harmony, that explains the plentiful forms of politeness that are so typical of Asian cultures. Harmony is also a key term when it comes to the Asian view of nature. While it is characteristic for the West to see nature primarily as something to be conquered, the concept of living in harmony with nature is characteristic in the East. In most Asian cultures bi-polar thought structures, such as *yin* and *yang*, prevail, and striving for a "middle road" is usually a high cultural value.

> In NCD, we strive to relate the characteristic insights of different cultures to each other.

My experiences:

One of the principles that guides my ministry is to focus on those elements that a given group most needs, rather than what the group most likes. When speaking in Western countries, for instance, I deliberately focus on the characteristics that Western churches are most lacking, incorporating the insights that we can gain from the Southern and Eastern parts of the world. The same holds true for ministry in Eastern or Southern countries. I am aware that this is contrary to how most people would do things. They would focus on the areas in which a given culture is already strong and would be happy about how "well received" their message was. But I see it as a waste of energy to travel thousands of miles just to tell people the very things at which they are already better than I.

Danger: Copying others

One of my Korean friends recently told me, "You Westerners have copyrights, while we Asians have a right to copy." This was meant as a joke, of course, but even with this joke he communicated an important cultural insight. Asian cultures can be great at copying others—in the positive sense. On the negative side, a "copy mentality" can result in a lack of individuality and a neglect of creativity.

As you know, in NCD the distinction between a model and a principle-oriented approach plays a central role. Without a doubt, the model-oriented approach has a stronger affinity to Eastern thought patterns, while the principle-oriented approach can be seen as a typically Western contribution to the worldwide discussion on church development. And I would explicitly like to add that this is a valuable contribution that will benefit non-Western cultures as well.

The South: Solidarity

What is a common denominator of the Southern hemisphere that encompasses such different parts of the world as Latin America and Africa? It's certainly not an accident that on these continents we find the two concepts of "liberation theology" and "African theology." In spite of all of their differences, these continents have one experience in common: suffering. Much of the way Africans and Latin Americans think has originated as a response to suffering. Among the Christians of the Southern hemisphere, we frequently encounter a high view of the Old Testament, creation, and the exodus as categories many people can identify with.

When looking for a common denominator that characterizes the South as a whole, the Xhosa word *ubuntu*, which Archbishop Desmond Tutu has placed at the center of his theology, seems to fit best. The concept of *ubuntu*, which is to a certain degree related to the Tanzanian *ujamaa* or the Kenyan *harambee*, is difficult to translate into a Western language. The closest equivalent that I have been able to come up with is the English term *solidarity*.

empirical research • principles

bi-polar thinking • all by itself

corporate profiles

cyclical thinking

Each feature of the NCD paradigm displayed in this diagram has an affinity to one of the three cultural poles. This explains why there are some aspects of NCD that people sense as "foreign." Usually, these are the very issues that are outside of their own cultural comfort zones and at the same time, reflect areas in which they most need to grow. It would be counterproductive to "contextualize them away" in order to make NCD more attractive to a given culture.

Ubuntu, however, is far more encompassing than solidarity. There is a famous saying in Xhosa, *Ubuntu ungamtu ngabanye abantu*, which can be transcribed to Western thought as follows: Each individual is ideally expressed in relation with others. Or: A person depends on other people to be a person. Or: You only recognize who you are in the mirror of relationship. This definitely expresses a form of group feeling and group loyalty that is virtually unknown to the Western world.

Ubuntu has a strong impact on Christianity. While in the Western world many believe that the individualistic approach to evangelism—God on the one hand, your soul on the other hand—is typically biblical, dealing with African or Latin American cultures helps us recognize that this focus on the individual is not typically biblical, but typically Western. The *koinonia* concept of the New Testament and the whole thought structure of the Old Testament, have a close affinity to *ubuntu*.

In the Southern hemisphere, we can detect cyclical ways of thinking that are in contrast to the linear thought structure of the West. Later in this book we will learn how valuable cyclical thinking is in the area of church development, and why cultures outside of the Southern hemisphere should strive to increase their competence in this area.

Danger: Conformity

Just as with the other cultural poles, there are limitations to the Southern thought pattern. A pre-occupation with group loyalty can lead to a neglect of personal freedom. It can result in a level of conformity that inhibits the development of people's full potential. And most importantly, it can undermine personal responsibility. If the forces of self-initiative aren't encouraged, the competitiveness of an entire economy suffers. In these areas, Southern cultures can learn from both the East and the West.

The impact on NCD

In Natural Church Development, we strive to integrate insights from all three cultural poles, and to avoid their pitfalls. The diagram at the top of page 31 shows that each element of the NCD paradigm has an affinity to one of the three cultural poles.

If you are a Westerner, you will most likely have more difficulty with cyclical thinking or "all by itself" growth than your brothers and sisters in the South or the East. The same holds true the other way around. People from non-Western cultures may find it more difficult than Westerners to relate empirical research to church life. There are elements in NCD that will seem more familiar to you, since your culture has prepared you for them, and there are others that will seem relatively "foreign" to you, since they are outside of your cultural comfort zone.

What globalization should be all about

The diagram on page 31 shows that the lacking aspects of a specific culture are provided by the other cultures. That is the major reason why NCD strives to develop a truly intercultural approach. It can be demonstrated that the very answers that are so greatly needed in the churches of one culture have usually already been found in another culture. As long as there is no cultural exchange—or, even worse, an exclusively one-way cultural export—we will never be able to benefit from this reality.

There is a widespread misconception that confuses globalization with the Westernization of the world. This would be nothing other than a form of cultural colonialism without weapons. The true meaning of the term globalization, however, is the opposite: In the global village all cultures learn from one another, all give and all receive. It has been one of the most enjoyable experiences of my life that seeing the world function like this has already become a reality within the worldwide NCD Community.

> Globalization shouldn't mean that one culture dominates the rest, but that all learn from each other.

More on the web:

On the internet (see page 162) you will find answers to the following questions:

- *In which culture does NCD work best?*

- *What are the political implications of the inter-cultural approach of NCD?*

Which cultural contributions mentioned in this chapter should you explore more?

NCD in an age of hype

Having worked for newspapers for a number of years, I am familiar with the laws of the media. I am aware of the kind of messages that create hype, and the kind that are regarded as irrelevant. The very things that keep the world going usually don't find their way into the media. They don't make for great stories. After all, news is what is different.

When starting our NCD network, we made the decision to ignore the laws of hype: no moving stories, no mass events, no model churches, no one-liners. Many people regarded this as a strategic mistake. A Christian leader told me, "Reality is what is going on in the media. If you are not present in the media, you are simply not a part of reality." I had to disagree. "Reality," I said, "is not what is going on in the media. Reality is what happens in reality, whether or not the media report on it." Many people are so infected by the reality-is-what-happens-in-the-media perspective that they only believe that they are alive if they read it in the newspaper!

Focus on changing reality

I am aware, of course, that people's view of reality is strongly influenced by the media, and not so much by reality itself. But what is our goal? To change reality, or just to change people's perception of reality? When seriously reflecting on this question, we made an even firmer commitment to invest all of our energies into long-term, principle-oriented, process-based activities—relatively boring to communicate, but incredibly exciting to be a part of.

A journalist is not very interested in how things *normally* function, but in the exceptions to the rule. News is what is different! Let's assume there is a relatively small church that meets in private homes. No extraordinary programs, no church buildings, no full-time staff. Year after year this church applies the principles of church development and experiences steady growth as a result. It even gives birth to four new congregations with about 15 people each. A fantastic *reality*—but not *news*.

The "mega" trap

Now consider a megachurch with a spectacular program, large buildings, and efficient PR. Even if this church displays only an average quality (according to the NCD Survey) and has been stagnating numerically for years, the media would be more interested in this church than in the one previously mentioned. That is normal, and as a journalist I understand such dynamics well. This church might even be labeled "a growing church" (confusing size with growth) and we

The very things that keep the world going usually don't find their way into the media.

My experiences:

A denominational leader in Canada once told me that he likes to send pastors of large churches with low quality to do apprenticeships with pastors of small, high-quality churches. One pastor of a 1,200 person church did an apprenticeship in a small church of 65 people. When he applied what he learned to his own church he experienced great results. Many people think this is a joke, but actually, this kind of procedure should be the most natural thing in the world. It can be demonstrated that applying principles to a larger church that have been learned in a smaller church is far easier than the other way around. It's exclusively the "mega" trap ("bigger is better") that doesn't allow for these learning experiences to happen more often.

might read about its high "quality" (confusing quality with professionalism). The laws of hype! "Mega" events are easier to sell than background processes. In the area of news this is a principle, in the area of church development it is a trap. I call it the "mega" trap.

Are larger churches better churches?

Don't misunderstand me. I am not opposed to *communicating* church-related activities in ways that are appealing to the media. Media support can create a "tail wind" that is helpful for advancing the kingdom of God. But I am very much opposed to focusing our energies on *creating* the kind of reality that appeals to the media. Following that approach, we unconsciously transfer the laws of hype, including the "mega" trap, to the dynamics of church development. And this is what has actually happened. Many Christians are already so deeply embedded in the "mega" trap that they seriously believe that the things the media take notice of are what is most effective for the kingdom of God.

Let me illustrate. One of the most controversial results of our initial NCD research in 32 countries and one thousand churches was that, on average, smaller churches are "better" churches (i.e. churches with measurably higher quality). There are, of course, countless exceptions to the rule, but the rule is this: The larger a church becomes, the worse its quality. The diagram on page 35 presents one example of these dynamics. I could add countless others. Whether we are dealing with the quality of relationships, giving habits, the intensity of prayer, or evangelistic outreach, smaller churches rank considerably higher, on average, than larger ones.

Small churches grow 1600% more

The situation gets even more dramatic when we compare the growth patterns of small and large churches. When we compared all of the churches with less than 100 regular attenders (the average size being 51 worshippers) with all of the churches that have a regular attendance of more than 1,000 (the average being 2,856), the result was striking. We discovered that "small churches" grow 16 times more than megachurches.

When doing such a comparison, we could not compare *one* church of 51 people to *one* of 2,856. We had to compare the results of 56 churches of 51 people each, to one megachurch with 2,856 people to come up with exactly the same number of people, just differently organized. On average, the small church category had a 1,600% higher growth rate. They won 16 times as many people! Interesting results, aren't they? Small churches really have no reason for a low self-esteem.

> Some people only believe that they are alive if they read it in the newspaper.

More on the web:

On the internet (see page 162) you will find answers to the following questions:

• *What are the reasons that larger churches tend to have lower quality?*

• *What are the unique contributions that large churches make to the body of Christ?*

Decreasing quality in larger churches

What percentage of the worshipping congregation uses their gifts to help the church grow?

31% — <100
29% — 100-200
26% — 200-300
24% — 300-1000
17% — >1000

worship attendance

This diagram illustrates the influence of church size on one of many aspects of church quality, namely the use of gifts. The percentage of people who use their gifts to help the church grow tends to decrease dramatically with church size. Whereas in churches with less than 100 people, 31% of the attenders use their gifts, in churches with more than 1000 people, only 17% use their gifts.

Overcoming low self-esteem

But here comes the tragic part of the story. In spite of this empirical evidence, many small churches have an incredibly low self-esteem that has inhibited further growth. I was in touch with one of these churches in Denmark. Their average attendance was 40. "There is not much happening in our church, no new people," the pastor, who worked part-time in a secular business, told me. I asked him how many people had joined the church within the past twelve months. He said, "Only four, but two others left the church." Well, that really didn't sound like an impressive growth rate. "And how many people did you have five years ago?" I asked. "Oh, about the same number," he said, "about 20."

Did you catch what he said? Their church went from 20 to 40 people in five years! If a megachurch of 20,000 grew at that rate, it would have 40,000 attenders in just five years. I don't know if there has ever been a church with such radical numbers, but if there ever should be, I can guarantee that the media would report on "one of the greatest revivals" ever. Now let's go back to our small church in Denmark with its frustrated part-time pastor: They had just experienced the exact same rate of growth that in the other case would be labeled a "mega revival." And yet they had such an incredible inferiority complex. If NCD could help those churches build healthy self-esteem, I think we will have done a fine job.

In what ways do you sense yourself to be influenced by the "mega trap"?

Who is your hero: David or Goliath?

The "mega" trap mentioned in the previous paragraph strongly impacts how we view and measure spiritual results. The danger is that, in the end, we aren't looking for real results any more, because we believe that a large infrastructure *is* the desired result.

How do we typically measure success?

When Christian organizations report on their success (I am speaking of para-church organizations, not local churches), they usually refer to items such as those listed in the upper box of the diagram on page 37:

> People don't admire Goliaths because they are more effective, but for the sheer fact that they are Goliaths.

- They give you a financial breakdown of the **money** that has been raised and spent, obviously under the assumption that the more money raised and spent, the more effective the ministry.

- They speak about the **time** that people have invested into different activities (the assumption being that the more time, the better).

- They tell you how many **workers** were employed (the more workers, the more successful the program).

- They let you know if the **organization** has expanded (the larger the organization, the greater the blessing).

- And, finally, they give you the numbers of the people that have been **evangelized and discipled**.

A new look at effectiveness

However, are these points really adequate indicators of spiritual success? In my view, only the last point ("people evangelized and discipled," where the criteria of a "disciple" includes the dimension of caring for the poor and needy) qualifies as a true, spiritual result. All of the other items are means to the end of achieving this result. Take a look at the two boxes labeled A and B. What most people fail to do is distinguish between *results* (box B) and *measures to achieve a result* (box A). Only when the size of box A contributes to a proportionally larger box B can we say that the measures to achieve a result are successful.

Let's assume that 25,000 people have participated in a Christian campaign. According to the categories in our diagram, would this be a result (box B) or would it be a measure to achieve a result (box A)? Very clearly it is a measure to achieve a result, a description of the investment, of the cost, so to speak. The decisive question is: What has been achieved by this enormous investment of time? If one year after the campaign the quality of the church has measurably increased and more people than before have found Christ and joined the church, we could rightly label this as a "result" (box B).

My experiences:

At the end of every year I ask the following questions: In which areas can we reduce the size of our organization? What ministries would be better taken care of by others? How can I reduce my personal involvements? I ask these questions because I am interested in contributing to "mega results." But what I am not interested in is building a "mega organization" that is promoted as the result.

A new look at effectiveness

What are spiritual results?

- money raised
- time spent
- workers employed
- organizations enlarged
- people evangelized & discipled

Measures to achieve a result

- money raised
- time spent
- workers employed
- organizations enlarged

Results

- people evangelized & discipled

The upper box shows some features that many Christian organizations would label as "success." A number of people, however, don't distinguish between "results" (box B) and "measures to achieve a result" (box A). Metaphorically speaking, they regard a large box A as an evidence of success.

Confusing boxes A and B

Large numbers of Christians continually confuse the two boxes. They innocently offer you the numbers of box A and cause you to believe that these are "results." Applying this logic, box A activities don't even have to justify themselves. Since a large box A results in an even larger box A, all we have to do is invest more energy into box A to enlarge box A. This is not a very helpful way of evaluating Christian organizations.

If we continued to follow this logic, meeting a goal with the participation of 20 employees would be superior to reaching the same goal with only one; winning 50 people to Christ with activities that cost $20,000 would be superior to winning the same number of people with activities that cost $300; and harvesting 10,000 potatoes with ten bags of fertilizer would be superior to getting the same number of potatoes with only one bag of fertilizer.

The ratio between A and B is the crucial factor

Let's translate this into the categories of our diagram. A large box A that corresponds to an average-size box B could hardly be considered a "successful infrastructure." However, if we had a tiny box A (only a small amount of money, time, workers, etc.) that corresponded to a large box B, we would have to call this a "super-successful infrastructure." In terms of success, it's neither the size of box A nor the size of box B that counts. Rather, the ratio between A and B is the crucial factor. It's amazing how few people apply this simple arithmetic. Is it possible that the "mega" trap mentioned earlier has impacted the way we do mathematics?

David and Goliath

When meditating on this diagram, the story of David and Goliath came to my mind. Many of us are not aware that this story is about two mutually exclusive approaches to life. Do we admire a *David approach* (large box B) or a *Goliath approach* (large box A)? When considering the biblical story, almost everyone answers "David," but in their daily lives they continue to admire the Goliaths of this world.

> The crucial factor is not how impressive you look, but what you actually achieve.

People admire Goliaths, not because they are more effective—in most cases, they aren't—but for the sheer fact that they are Goliaths. A Goliath doesn't have to justify himself, just as a large box A doesn't have to justify itself. But the crucial factor is not how impressive you look, but what you actually achieve. We should not forget that in the biblical story, Goliath was not "better equipped" than David. He was huge, that is true, but at the same time he was far too immobile to be a good fighter. David, on the other hand, fought with divine intelligence. He was better equipped to do his job than Goliath because God had given him all he needed. In NCD we are committed to following the David approach. We have worked hard to develop an approach that reaches the desired results with a minimum amount of infrastructure, at the lowest possible cost.

More on the web:

On the internet (see page 162) you will find answers to the following questions:

- *What is the difference between a "large organization" and a "Goliath organization"?*
- *How do "Goliath organizations" view NCD?*

In the past, which have you admired more, organizations that display a David, or a Goliath, approach?

Laughing at Goliath?

When I recently used the David-and-Goliath analogy in a conference in New Zealand, one of the participating leaders approached me and said, "You are absolutely right in what you have said, Christian, but you shouldn't say this in public." I was a little bit puzzled and asked, "Why?" He answered, "Because there are a number of Goliaths in this room that might have felt insulted. Typically they are admired by everyone, but now people may start to laugh at them." My reply was, "I agree with you that many people admire the Goliaths and laugh at the Davids. But if the two of us see this as a problem, our patterns of admiration and laughter have to change." When I first heard the story of David and Goliath—at that time I might have been five years old—I always laughed when I saw Goliath's picture in my Children's Bible. He looked almost ridiculous to me: Such a huge man, such huge armor, and such a poor outcome. Many of my friends reacted the other way around; they felt frightened when they saw Goliath's picture. I still think that I had a deeper understanding of the story than they did.

Why all of us need to check our "spiritual glasses"

Chapter 1

Whe speaking about the NCD paradigm, I frequently hear the comment, "That's theory. We have enough good theories. What we need is practice." I passionately disagree. In the area of church life, we definitely don't have enough good theories. It's true that we have a lot of *theories*, but most of them should not be labeled as "good." They are *bad* theories—theories that don't work.

What is the essence of a good theory? A good theory produces good fruit. And if we encounter bad fruit, there is very likely to be bad theory in the background.

The relationship between theory and practice

It can be demonstrated that, whether it is obvious or not, every good practice is based on good theory. A considerable part of our job in the Institute for Natural Church Development is to constantly analyze thousands of different "good practices" and to try to identify the "theory" that is behind them. The opposite holds true as well. Every bad practice is rooted in bad theory. We need to identify those theories so that we can tackle them. The alternative is not, "theory or practice," as some people want to make us believe. Rather it is, "good theories that produce good practices" or "bad theories that produce bad practices."

A theory can influence you whether you are thinking about it or not. In fact, the best way of applying a good theory is by intuition. If you have reached that stage, the theory has become part of you. You don't have to think about it any more; you simply follow your internal compass, which can be trusted, as it is a reflection of good (i.e. biblical, true, tested, fruit-producing) theory. However, if you have been influenced by a bad theory it's almost impossible to change your practice without reflective thought.

Everyone wears "spiritual glasses"

To tackle this theoretical side, we use the term "paradigms." Every single one of us, whether aware of it or not, is influenced by specific paradigms that can either help or hinder our approach to church development. The simplest way to understand how paradigms work in our lives is to compare them to spiritual glasses. You and I might look at exactly the same reality, we might even look at the same Bible verse, and yet see something completely different depending on the kind of glasses we wear.

If we are not aware of the fact that we have spiritual glasses, we are in danger of confusing reality with the colors that our

Many Christians are not even aware that they are wearing spiritual glasses.

My experiences:

At a National NCD Conference in South Africa, I decided to concentrate on the topic of "spiritual glasses." One of the participants complained publicly that this focus on paradigms was not practical enough for him. My response was, "Only a few years ago, in South Africa you had committed Christians on both sides of the apartheid system, such as President Botha and Archbishop Tutu. Both of them read their Bibles daily, but both of them drew very different conclusions out of it. Some of the black people even asked: 'Do the whites really have the same Bible that we do?' Of course they did. The difference was that they were reading it through different glasses. Please, never make the mistake of regarding this as an abstract, purely academic topic. World history has been shaped by the kind of glasses people wear."

glasses display. We might even wonder why our fellow Christians see something completely different when they deal with the same reality as we do.

A new relationship with God is not enough

Let's face it. The positions that we Christians take on some of the most crucial issues of today's world—human rights, violence, ecology, racism, genetic engineering, abortion, poverty, peace, world missions—are not so much determined by the intensity of our relationship to Christ nor by dealing with the "facts" themselves, but by the spiritual glasses we wear. Until we are aware of this fact, we will constantly be in danger of confusing these glasses (the world view we have adopted over time), with the "will of God." It's troubling how few Christians are even aware of these mental dynamics.

> If you are really interested in a paradigm shift, and not just in church cosmetics, you should thank God for times of crisis.

For this reason, it's crucial to help people find a personal relationship with God, but it is not enough. We also need to help them find the right pair of spiritual glasses. In academic language, this change of glasses is referred to as a "paradigm shift." Such a shift usually doesn't occur while sitting on a sunny garden terrace reading a book. In most cases, paradigm shifts are connected to times of crisis. If you are really interested in a paradigm shift, and not just in church cosmetics, you should thank God for times of crisis in your church.

The central importance of paradigms

I hope to convince you that the topic of paradigms is an eminently practical issue. It impacts the center of your whole belief system. It impacts your emotions. It impacts your theological preferences. It impacts your political views. It impacts your inner images of how the church should function. Scripture reminds us of the central importance of our mental paradigms: "As a man thinks in his heart, so he is" (Proverbs 23:7).

> Have there already been "paradigm shifts" in your own life? In the life of your church?

In order to tackle the question of spiritual glasses, in NCD we talk about the *Trinitarian Compass*. Chapter 2 (pages 44-79) deals exclusively with this compass and how you can practically use it in your personal life and in the life of your church. The wonderful thing about the Trinitarian Compass is that it doesn't try to push you into a direction that somebody else—such as I as the author of this book—has defined as important. Rather it helps you to move exactly into the direction that is important for *you*. The direction you have to take may be very different from the direction I have to take, as we may have very different starting points. Applying the Trinitarian Compass will enable you to view your own life and the life of other people through new glasses.

Information, application, trans- formation—what's needed most?

When it comes to learning the principles of Natural Church Development, it is helpful to distinguish the following three levels: information, application, and transformation. One of the most widespread traps I have encountered is the erroneous assumption that high competence in the area of informational acquisition automatically releases applicational know-how and transformational power.

Level 1: Information

Without a doubt, the information level is important. For that reason we have invested several years in this area. We wanted to learn what principles God uses worldwide to build his church. That is why we put so much energy into research. After we had collected sufficient data, we again invested a lot of energy in sharing this information with as many people as possible. Before we could deal with the question of *how* to teach things, we had to know *what* to teach. Before we could deal with the question of *how* to apply the principles, we had to know *what* the principles were. Without a solid basis of information, application and transformation don't work.

Therefore, I don't agree with the increasingly popular idea that downgrades the importance of information and strives to substitute it with "transformational learning." The information level is absolutely necessary, as it is the foundation for everything else.

However, being an information expert doesn't guarantee that you will be able to apply the information. Many churches have specialized in information that increases people's ability to answer why they do what they do; however, this does not necessarily improve their skills. Knowledge and know-how are two different aspects of learning. One does not automatically result in the other.

Level 2: Application

It's interesting to notice that people who routinely solve complex, real-life problems often have comparatively low IQs, revealing the fact that practical intelligence is different from theoretical intelligence. One of our NCD Partners did a revealing study of this concept. They developed a 25-question test that dealt with how to apply NCD principles to everyday life. On average, lay people answered 18 questions correctly, while pastors only got 11 answers right. Was this because the pastors were less "intelligent"? Certainly not. But the classical academic training that most of them had completed was primarily, if not exclusively, focused on theoretical, rather than practical, intelligence.

> Every human being is incredibly creative. However, this creative power has frequently been suppressed.

My experiences:

When speaking about the role of creativity in NCD, I am frequently told, "That doesn't work in our church. People need exact instructions of what to do, step by step. They simply are not that creative." Whenever I hear this, I ask: "What have you done in the past few years to train your people to release their God-given creativity? If you haven't consistently invested in this area, you should not complain that it doesn't work. Every human being is incredibly creative. Regretfully, in many churches this creative power has not been encouraged, and sometimes it has even been systematically suppressed. Could it be that your church is one of them?"

There are many people who operate well at the application level with little capacity at the information level. They simply do the right things, but have difficulty explaining why they do it that way. This pattern can be observed in countless churches where wonderful practice is not linked to any reflected-upon theoretical framework. It is actually possible to function at the application level without being strong at the information level. However, there is a danger of doing things this way. When leaders of these churches are asked about their secret of success, they often present a sort of theory that can be counterproductive for others. I have collected examples where even a clear *mistake*—that took place in the midst of a successful ministry—was promoted as a "key to success."

Information and application have to be put into balance. If we neglect either one of them, we will run into problems. For that reason, we have developed a number of NCD tools that are focused on integrating the two dimensions.

Level 3: Transformation

However, there is more than just information and application. Until the transformation level has been attained, all of our attempts at church development are in danger of remaining a rather uninspiring undertaking. Consider the following metaphor: At the information level you discover a tool, at the application level you learn how to use that tool, and at the transformation level you *become* a tool (more on page 148). Transformation opens the doors for a completely new dimension of effectiveness. You begin to radiate the very principles that you are trying to teach to others.

Notice that this is not a "three-step" program, but rather a never-ending cycle (see graphic on page 43). Let's assume that you have already gone through this cycle once. When you enter the information zone again, you will enter it as a different person with new experiences and questions. This integration of information, application, and transformation makes any learning process an adventure. Many people have a negative view of "learning," simply because they have never experienced this continuous, dynamic cycle of learning. In most cases, they are victims of an "information-only" approach.

Stimulating creativity

NCD is all about releasing the creativity that God has already implanted into every human being. We don't want you to play *our* musical scores. We want to empower you to compose *your own* beautiful music. The more times you have

---

> **NCD doesn't want you to play our musical scores, but empowers you to compose your own beautiful music.**

My experiences:

When I visited China for the first time, a pastor told me that he had known what we call the "eight quality characteristics of growing churches" long before we did our research to identify them. "How is that possible?", I asked him. He told me, "I can smell the eight quality characteristics in a church. Each of them radiates a certain atmosphere that you can detect even without research." When this pastor is asked to help other churches, he sends teams whose primary task is simply to radiate what he calls the "eight atmospheres." That's clearly a kind of learning that goes beyond the information and application levels. It is transformational learning in action.

This illustration highlights the three levels of learning: the high school student as a symbol for collecting information, the doctor as a symbol for applying information to practice, and the priest as a symbol for the transformation of a whole life.

gone through a learning cycle like the one we have been talking about here, the more you will be aware of how creative you are.

Transformation and the Trinitarian Compass

The intention of this book is to lead you into all three dimensions of learning. On the next pages, you will find a lot of *information* that I share with you for just one reason: I am convinced that these pieces of information will be essential for you in your attempts to grow personally and as a whole church. I have taken great care to justify every statement I make, as I believe that any reader deserves not only to know my conclusions, but also the thought processes that brought me to them. Throughout the book, you will be encouraged to *apply* that knowledge, both to your own life and to the life of your church.

However, *Color Your World with Natural Church Development* wants to lead you beyond information and application. It wants to help you proceed to the level of transformation. That is the major reason why I have given the Trinitarian Compass such a predominant role throughout the book. It's basically an instrument of transformation.

According to your NCD knowledge, which of the three levels describes you best?

The Trinitarian Compass

2

Natural Church Development is not a marketing gimmick to get more people to attend church. Rather, it is built around a spiritual compass that helps you experience God in his fullness—especially those aspects of God's nature you have yet to discover. At the same time, it enables you to view the world through new lenses. Once you have learned how to utilize the Trinitarian Compass, you will clearly see where you need to grow in your relationship to God. You will also understand why other believers think, feel, and act very differently than you, and how the steps that are important for your spiritual growth might be inappropriate or even counterproductive for others.

Chapter 2

My personal "trinitarian pilgrimage"

I n a recent interview, I was asked, "What do you believe people will connect with your name 50 years from now?" I didn't have to think about my answer. "I don't believe that it will be the term Natural Church Development," I said. "It will very likely be the Trinitarian Compass." I am convinced that in the future, a large number of Christians around the world will be fully involved with the "three-color" approach. Why? Because they will sense that the concept behind the colors green, red, and blue will bring exactly the kind of biblical balance that they are looking for.

Each color I discovered enabled me to see things that I hadn't noticed before.

The Trinitarian Compass did not emerge as an instrument for analyzing my own life. However, when looking back at my own pilgrimage as a Christian, I can clearly see how God has gradually brought each of the three colors of the Compass to my attention.

Red: Focus on evangelism & discipleship

The day that I came to know Christ personally was overwhelming to me. I was discipled in a congregation that today I would call a "red church." It had a clear evangelical focus. However, it was free of any legalistic tendencies that are so often encountered in churches of that color, and I thank God for that. It became crystal clear to me that I had to invest the rest of my life in helping other people find a personal relationship with God. It was as if he was telling me, "Christian, never forget what I have done for you. I erased your sin. My friend, share this discovery with as many people as you can."

Green: Focus on tolerance & social justice

As a young believer I got involved with Christian groups that had a strong focus on peace, ecology, reconciliation, and social justice. Together, we participated in various forms of social action. The wonderful thing about these "green groups" was that they showed no tendency to relativism or syncretism, which is a frequent tendency in the green color zone. It was as if God was telling me, "Christian, never forget my passion for all of my creation, and especially for the poor. If you should ever bypass this concern in your ministry, my heart will cry out."

I had now made two spiritual discoveries, I had a great vision of what to do for the rest of my life, and I had a problem. On my 18th birthday, I had been diagnosed with an incurable kidney disease that limited my life-expectancy drastically. This realization brought an enormous sense of urgency to my life. While my friends lived it up at their weekend parties, I volunteered at a newspaper in order to learn how to write. While others took their summer vacations, I learned foreign

My experiences:

When people ask me, "What theology is at the root of NCD?", I usually refer to my book "Paradigm Shift in the Church," which addresses that question in 280 pages and 676 footnotes. A frequent reply is, "I have read that book, but I still have doubts. Are you a full-blooded evangelical? A charismatic? Maybe a liberal?" I respond by refusing to give myself or NCD any of those labels. To do so would force me to defend everything that others who have been put into the same box, have ever written or said. "But we need one word that summarizes your theology," people tell me. My answer is, "If you really need one word, take this one: trinitarian." NCD is a trinitarian approach to church growth. That term summarizes my personal theology as well.

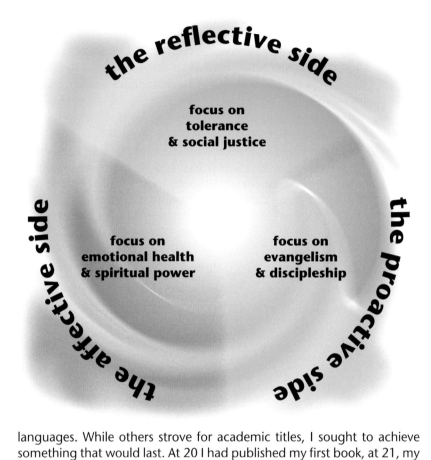

the reflective side

focus on
tolerance
& social justice

the affective side

focus on
emotional health
& spiritual power

focus on
evangelism
& discipleship

the proactive side

Throughout the course of my own life, God has gradually brought all three colors to my attention. It took some time before I realized that having all three colors in balance is the secret both to church development and personal growth.

languages. While others strove for academic titles, I sought to achieve something that would last. At 20 I had published my first book, at 21, my second. With a short life one has to work more quickly than the rest!

Blue: Focus on emotional health & spiritual power

Eight years after the disease had been diagnosed, I was healed through prayer. That was probably the deepest emotional experience of my life, and it was my personal introduction to the "blue zone." That day I redesigned my life. The Christians who helped me grow in the blue zone were down-to-earth people, free of all "spiritualizing" tendencies that can so often be found in charismatic groups. It was as if God was telling me, "Christian, it was my desire that you get to know my supernatural power firsthand. Never forget this dimension, whatever you do in ministry."

In my own pilgrimage, I have had three significant encounters with the same God, but each time I got to know different aspects of who he is. Each color that I discovered enabled me to see things that I hadn't noticed before. When God led me to the concept of the Trinitarian Compass, it not only helped me to understand Christianity around the world better, but it also helped me to understand my own life.

Which "colors" have been most influential in your personal pilgrimage?

The center of theology

I have attended a number of church growth seminars at which I learned a lot about marketing, communication, fund-raising, and organizational skills. The seminars contained valuable pieces of information, but they had nothing at all to do with the essence of the church. I could have learned exactly the same things in secular management seminars.

I have also attended countless theological seminars that focused on the secret of the Trinity. What I learned was, without a doubt, important for understanding Christian doctrine, but I didn't sense any impact on my everyday life. In one situation, I looked into the eyes of every individual participant and realized that the following Monday each one of them would return to their ordinary routine of activities, whether or not they had attended the seminar. Our minds had been illuminated, but our hearts and hands had not been affected in any significant way.

With the same key, we can unlock some of the deepest secrets of both theology and everyday life.

Theology and practice

I have found both kinds of experiences equally confusing. The very things that were focused on our daily lives had nothing to do with theology, and theology had nothing to do with our daily lives. Does it really have to be that way?

In Natural Church Development, the theological compass is the same as the practical compass. In other words, the theology behind NCD permeates even the most practical aspects of church life. There is no schizophrenia between theology and practice. It is possible to unlock, with the same key, some of the deepest secrets of both theology and everyday life.

Not just for Sundays

When I do a seminar on the Trinitarian Compass, I tell the participants at the outset, "Once you start to apply the dynamics of the Trinitarian Compass, your life will be changed. You will do different things next Monday, Tuesday, Wednesday, and maybe even Sunday. However, the focus of the Trinitarian compass is not on Sunday, it is on the other six days of the week."

What is the secret of the Trinitarian Compass? In essence, it is this: Drawing closer to the living God. That brings balance and health, power and wisdom, depth and open-mindedness to a church. It releases what we call "all by itself" growth. It attracts people from the outside, as they sense that there is a magnetic power in such a church. They feel drawn into this magnetic field, even before they realize that God is the source of that power. And one of the results within such a church is numerical growth, even if that term had never been used throughout the whole process.

My experiences:

People ask me why the Trinitarian Compass was not in the original NCD book. The only answer I can give is that at the time of writing that book, that instrument was not yet available to me. Even when I wrote the first book about the Trinitarian Compass, I had no idea what kind of role it would later play in NCD.

What would you define as the center of theology?

You can reflect God's light

I have placed the metaphor of "light" at the very center of my book, *The 3 Colors of Love*. Jesus not only called *himself* "the light of the world" (John 8:12), he also used the same terminology in his Sermon on the Mount to describe his disciples: *they* are "the light of the world" (Mt. 5:14). Metaphorically speaking, Jesus is the sun, his disciples are the moon. Both shed light, so the effect is similar. However, the sun is the source of the light, and the moon merely reflects the light that it receives from the sun. When we see the "moonlight" at night, we should never forget that we are still seeing the "light of the sun."

God is light

While in many religions the metaphor of light has been used in highly speculative ways, it is characteristic of biblical teaching to be devoid of any esoteric connotations. John, in particular, uses the imagery of light and darkness throughout his writings, culminating in the sentence, "God is light, and in him there is no darkness at all" (1 John 1:5). Thus we are challenged to "believe in the light" and to become "sons of the light" ourselves (John 12:36), which means no more nor less than to reflect the divine light in our own lives.

It is certainly no coincidence that the first thing God created was light (Gen. 1:3). Light is one of the preconditions of life. It illuminates, reveals truth, destroys illusions, and shows us the path we must take. Darkness is nothing other than the absence of light. It doesn't have any power of its own. How can we fight against the manifestations of darkness, such as sin and heresy? By spreading the light! Where light shines, darkness has no place. It disappears "all by itself."

Probably the most practical implication of understanding God as "light" is the clear revelation of our job description as Christians. We are to reflect the divine light. The Bible speaks about "walking in the light" (1 John 1:7). The Christian mystics used the image of a mirror to communicate this truth: A mirror can only reflect when it has first been cleaned. This is the backdrop for the many "purification" practices that we find among these groups: to become a more effective mirror for reflecting God's light.

The colors of light

What is light? In God's creation, light is nothing other than color. It is important to notice that the colors of light (self-luminous colors) function differently than object colors. When we mix object colors (such as oil or water colors), the presence of all of the colors is black, while the absence of all color is white—an empty canvas. Self-luminous colors function the other way around: the presence of all colors is white, while black is the

Our task is not to produce light, but to reflect the divine light.

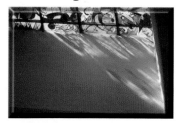

My experiences:

It makes a great difference to know that my job is not to create light, but to reflect God's light. Since I am aware that I am unable to reflect the fullness of God's light on my own, I am eager to minister alongside fellow-Christians who reflect those colors of God's light that I don't reflect clearly enough.

To display a photograph on a computer screen, the colors red, green, and blue are needed. Only when all three are present do we get a precise picture of reality.

absence of any color. In the color white, the whole spectrum of light is reflected. The brighter the light, the more powerful the reflection.

Those of us who do our work on computers experience these dynamics every day, since that is how images are projected on a computer screen. In order to display a picture in full color, the screen has to project red, green, and blue. If one color is missing, the image is distorted (see diagram at the top of this page). These dynamics are not a human invention. They simply express how the colors of light, that God has created, function.

Light and the Trinitarian Compass

What feelings does the image of being a "mirror" of God's light stimulate in you?

The Trinitarian Compass seeks to express these dynamics. Just as light passing through a prism fans out into the different colors of the spectrum, the light of God can be reflected by us in various ways. Some people might reflect green, others red, others blue—yet we all reflect the same God. The metaphor also makes it clear that as long as our view of God is only restricted to one or two of the three colors, it is not complete. It is a constant challenge for every believer to broaden his or her experience to the color(s) we do not yet reflect.

How God communicates with you

As illuminating as the metaphor of light may be, the Trinitarian Compass has a richer background: God's threefold revelation that is expressed by the names Father, Son, and Holy Spirit in the classical formulations of the fourth century. I have tried to express this in the diagram on page 53, but have deliberately chosen terms that don't refer to the relationship that the three persons of the Godhead have *to each other,* but to the relationship that *we* have with God.

It is characteristic of all three revelations that God not only reveals "something" of himself, but himself. This applies to the "creation revelation" (the green zone of the diagram), as well as to the "salvation revelation" (red zone), and to the "personal revelation" (blue zone). It is important that we understand the specific character of each of these three revelations.

The "creation revelation"

God revealed himself as Creator by leaving the marks of his character on creation (Ps. 19:2; Rom. 1:19f). One does not have to be a Christian in order to encounter this type of revelation *(green zone).* Whether you are a Muslim, Buddhist, atheist, or Christian, when you turn to creation you can see the fingerprints of the Creator. This type of revelation is truly interreligious.

When making such a statement we must keep in mind that it describes the creation revelation, not the salvation revelation or the personal revelation. It is evident that the creation revelation can be understood in different ways and can also be misunderstood. On the basis of this form of revelation alone, no one will come to the realization that the Creator is the father of Jesus Christ.

The "salvation revelation"

The salvation revelation *(red zone)* has a different character. Jesus is the one in whom we definitely see God for who he really is (John 14:9). In Christ, God became man, in him "all the fullness of the Deity lives in bodily form" (Col. 2:9). He is the one who reconciles us with God (2 Cor. 5:19). According to the New Testament, our relationship to Jesus Christ determines our salvation or damnation (Acts 4:12). Through him we receive "eternal life" (Rom. 6:23).

The "personal revelation"

I refer to the personal revelation *(blue zone)* as the time when what God did for us objectively in Christ becomes a personal, subjective reality. Through the Holy Spirit, "Christ for us" becomes "Christ in us" (Gal. 2:20, 4:19;

God's revelation always aims at establishing a relationship.

My experiences:

The introduction of the Trinitarian Compass has made NCD relevant for churches of diverse theological backgrounds such as evangelicals, charismatics, and liberals. Naturally, evangelicals have a strong affinity to the color red; charismatics, to blue; and liberals, to green. The Trinitarian Compass enables each of them to appreciate their areas of strengths, and at the same time to grow in those areas where they are not yet strong. To see this happen in thousands of churches, is one of the most exhilarating aspects of my ministry.

Col. 1:27). Through the Holy Spirit, God pours his love into our hearts (Rom. 5:5). God's Spirit enters into a relationship with our spirit. Thus a human being can literally become "the temple of the Holy Spirit" (1 Cor. 6:19). The revelation of the Holy Spirit is the revelation in our hearts. It happens, for example, when a person becomes a Christian (1 Cor. 12:3). If this personal appropriation does not take place, the revelation of God has not achieved its goal.

A threefold response

God's revelation always aims at establishing a relationship. In all three revelations we encounter the one, true God, but each time we encounter him in a different way. His threefold communication with us, which should correspond to a threefold response on our part, is fundamental to the nature of God as revealed to us in the Bible. Whenever one of the three dimensions is neglected, we have an incomplete experience of God. Most of the problems that we experience in the everyday life of our churches are, in the final analysis, based on an incomplete understanding of the threefold revelation of God.

Impact on all areas

Nobody can recognize the nature of radium if he or she does not understand its effect: radioactivity. In a similar way, nobody will be able to comprehend the nature of God if he or she does not understand his deeds. The reality of God is revealed to us through his actions. In the four small diagrams at the bottom of this page I have tried to link the threefold revelation of God with various theological themes.

> No one can comprehend the nature of God without understanding his deeds.

- The *first* image indicates the most immediate consequence of the threefold revelation of God: the green zone is designated for creation; the red zone, for salvation; and the blue zone, for sanctification. In all three cases, it is the same God (white center) who does the work. At the same time each of these three works of God can be related to one of the three forms of revelation.

Three works

creation
salvation
sanctification

Three locations

God above us
God among us
God in us

Three appeals

You shall!
You may!
You can!

Three authorities

science
Scripture
experience

God is not only perceived by humans in different ways, he has also revealed himself to us in a threefold way: creation revelation (green zone), salvation revelation (red zone), and personal revelation (blue zone).

• The *second* image expresses three different "locations" where God meets us: The eternal God, whom we know is "above us" (green zone), through the incarnation of Jesus Christ lives "among us" (red zone), and at the same time produces the knowledge of his presence "within us" (blue zone). The one, true God can be encountered in all three places.

• The *third* image sketches three practical consequences for our life. The three revelations of God embody the appeal ("You shall!", green zone), the invitation ("You may!", red zone), and the empowerment ("You can!", blue zone). None of these three appeals should be neglected in church life. Only those who have come to know God in all three ways will be able to serve him according to his plan.

• The *fourth* image relates the same threeness to three authorities that guide each of us: science (green zone), Scripture (red), and experience (blue). It should be clear that these three sources of knowledge are not given the same value (not every source produces an adequate knowledge of God), and yet we can encounter the fingerprints of God in each area. Neglecting one of these areas has serious consequences.

Which color zone is, right now, the area of your greatest experience with God?

Chapter 2

Let's strive for spiritual balance

T he message behind the Trinitarian Compass is the message of spiritual balance. As all three color zones are equally important, the constant challenge is to identify which one is least developed. When you focus on strengthening that area, you automatically contribute to greater balance. This applies to you as an individual as well as to your small group, to your church, and to your whole denomination. There is always one area that is less developed than the other two and demands your special attention.

> A balanced life, according to biblical standards, is something radical.

My experiences:

Our software that helps groups identify their color profiles in the area of gift-based ministry was released the day I was doing an NCD seminar in the United States. Dave Wetzler, our American NCD Partner, suggested we spontaneously demonstrate to the participants how it works. So I input my data—an imbalanced profile with a strong tendency to the "left." Afterwards, Dave input his data—just as imbalanced a profile, but this time with a tendency to the "right." Then Dave pressed the "corporate profile" button, and at that moment the computer revealed a wonderfully balanced result. Completely unplanned, the result was a powerful demonstration for all of us of how the body of Christ functions.

Radical balance

When speaking about "balance," I have made an interesting discovery. This focus is usually well received, but in many cases the popularity of the theme is based on a serious misunderstanding. For many people "balance" is almost synonymous with anything that is not radical: yielding an equally low level of commitment in all three color zones—only a little bit green, only a little bit red, and only a little bit blue.

Within the Trinitarian Compass, however, we try to apply a biblical model of balance—to be as committed as possible in all three areas: radically Christ-centered (red zone), radically ministering in the power of the Holy Spirit (blue zone), and radically focused on God's creation (green zone). The concept of balance should never become an excuse for a lack of commitment. We must pursue "radical balance."

My own imbalance

I am working hard at applying these dynamics to my own life. Using the categories of the diagram on page 55, in many areas of my life I display what we could call an "imbalance to the left." Personally, I am very much influenced by emotions, dreams, and relationships (all typical characteristics of the left pole in our diagram). When it comes to crucial decisions in my life, this dimension usually affects me far more than rational proof, financial considerations, or empirical facts.

The reason why I focus so much on the green zone (research, deductive reasoning) and on the red zone (Scripture, practical implementation) reflects my personal attempt to bring balance to my life. People who only know me superficially misunderstand this and sometimes believe I am a cold-blooded rationalist who is only interested in getting results. The very opposite is far more accurate. However, if I didn't stress the "right pole," I would actually be in danger of being completely absorbed by the blue zone in an unbalanced, unhealthy, and unbiblical way.

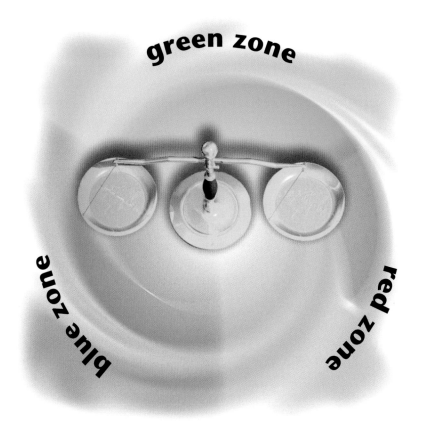

green zone

blue zone

red zone

As each color zone is equally important, the challenge is to bring all of them into balance. This demands that we constantly evaluate how strongly developed each of the three areas is.

Individual imbalance—corporate balance

I am aware that all of us, as long as we live on this earth, will be out of balance. Even if you strive hard to bring more balance to your life—and you certainly should—you will never fully succeed, since you are not Jesus. However, what you can do is network with other believers who have imbalances in the opposite directions. Together you can reflect God's light far more completely than you could on your own. In order to see this happen, however, you have to resist the tendency to be exclusively surrounded by people with the same "color profile" as your own.

Later in this chapter (pages 74-79) you will find the NCD Color Profile, an instrument that will help you identify which color zone you personally should focus on, and which one should be the focus of your whole church. The goal of that test is far more than to provide a program for spiritual self-discovery. The Color Profile is all about pursuing radical balance in the life of your church. Before you decide which color area to focus on, you need to know which one has been most neglected in the past.

Right now, would you consider your life to be in balance or does it tend in a certain direction?

The New Jerusalem— descending to earth

Scripture uses a plethora of images to communicate the message of bringing all three colors (or better, what the colors hint at) into balance. In fact, once you have developed "trinitarian glasses" (in contrast to mono-colored glasses that only allow you to see the green or red or blue dimensions), you will be astonished by how consistently the Bible reminds us of this theme.

> Once you have caught the vision of manifesting all three dimensions in your life, the New Jerusalem has descended into your heart.

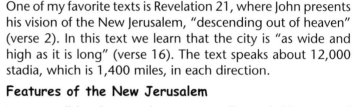

One of my favorite texts is Revelation 21, where John presents his vision of the New Jerusalem, "descending out of heaven" (verse 2). In this text we learn that the city is "as wide and high as it is long" (verse 16). The text speaks about 12,000 stadia, which is 1,400 miles, in each direction.

Features of the New Jerusalem

It may well be that you have repeatedly read this text and maybe even preached on it, without noticing what the New Jerusalem is all about:

• It expresses **God's ideal** that is revealed to us, not for spiritual entertainment, but for a specific purpose.

• It has **three dimensions**: width, height, and depth.

• Each of these three dimensions has the **same size**.

• It's the **balance** of the three dimensions that constitutes the perfection of the city.

• The size of every single dimension is incredibly **large** (1,400 miles).

• The size of the city is **measured** (verse 16) in order to identify its equilibrium.

• **God approaches us** in the city that fulfills those criteria. The glory of God (verse 11), even God himself (verse 3), dwells in it; he gives light to this city (verse 23).

Impact on everyday life

These statements are metaphors, of course, just as our Trinitarian Compass is a metaphor. However, the images are so clear that I wonder why many people have difficulty with this text. Could it be that many of us are so pre-occupied with reading it as a description of life after death that we are in danger of missing its relevance for our lives here and now? By giving us the vision of the New Jerusalem, God definitely wants to impact our lives. It's our task as individuals to bring our lives into harmony with that vision. It's our task as churches to bring our churches' lives into harmony with that vision. It's our task as denominational leaders to bring our denominations into harmony with that vision.

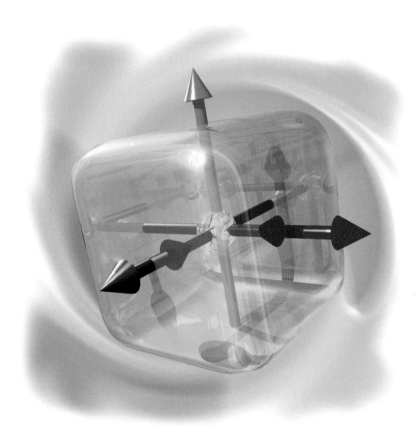

In the book of Revelation, the New Jerusalem is described to be "as wide and high as it is long" (Rev. 21: 16). These three dimensions communicate the same thing that we try to express with the Trinitarian Compass. The red arrow symbolizes width; the green arrow, height; and the blue arrow, length or depth.

The most important dimension

Which of the three dimensions is most important: the height, the width, or the depth? Taking the ideal of "radical balance" seriously, there is only one possible answer: It's the very dimension that is, right now, the least developed. Only by focusing on that "minimum factor" can we expect to bring balance both to our personal lives and to the lives of our churches. Sometimes people ask me for a biblical reference to the "minimum factor strategy" that plays an important role in NCD (see pages 124-145). They would like me to show them the *term* "minimum factor" in one of the biblical books, rather than realizing that the biblical *focus on balance* inevitably results in focusing on the areas that are least developed.

Is this text about life after death or about our lives here and now? As so much in Scripture, it's about both. As long as you live in this world, you won't be able to see the New Jerusalem in its fullness. But once you have caught the vision of manifesting all three dimensions in your life, the New Jerusalem has descended into your heart. Too many interpreters of this text want to keep the New Jerusalem in heaven, rather than realizing that the "descending out of heaven" is the crucial point.

Have you ever related the New Jerusalem to the concept of spiritual balance before?

Chapter 2

Why Christianity is in such a bad state today

S ince God has revealed to us such a wonderful paradigm for how his church should function and has empowered us with everything we need to put it into practice, we seriously have to ask why it so often doesn't work. My conclusion is that we human beings have an incurable tendency to choose one of the three colors as our "favorite color," rather than to strive to integrate all three dimensions into the lives of our churches.

One of the responsibilities of leadership is to constantly identify areas of imbalance.

My experiences:

Since my ministry leads me into very diverse groups, I constantly have to deal with imbalances and even heresies. It has been helpful for me to realize that there are heresies in all three color segments, not just in one or two of them. Whereas in liberal groups (green zone) the danger of relativism can frequently be detected, in many evangelical groups (red zone) the danger of legalism is prevalent. Similarly, many charismatic groups (blue zone) have problems with a spiritualizing world view that conflicts with God's creation and biblical standards. By encouraging all of them to grow into their "opposite" color segments, I try to help them overcome their core problems.

Heresy = a partial truth

Take a look at the diagram on page 59. As you can see, each of the three colors is related to a specific danger that inevitably occurs at the moment the other two colors are neglected. In other words, the best way to avoid the three dangers mentioned in the diagram is to strengthen the "opposite color zones."

Heresy is not, as many of us believe, the opposite of the truth. In most cases it is something far more delicate. It's a *partial* truth. There is always a grain of truth in any heresy. However, since it is not integrated into the other aspects of truth, but presented as an absolute, it becomes a partial truth and thus a heresy. Every teaching can become heretical, if elements of the truth—no matter how biblical they are—are regarded as the whole truth. In almost every single case, heretical groups are biblically right in the very aspects they stress. But they are wrong in neglecting countless other aspects of the biblical message. It's a tragedy that, throughout church history, things have only rarely been analyzed in this way.

The three core dangers

We have already seen that the reflective side (green segment) is essential for a healthy understanding of the Christian faith. However, if that dimension is isolated and set up as an absolute, we end up with **rationalism**, which is—in contrast to rationality—a real danger for the Christian church. Or look at the red area, the proactive side—another essential dimension of the Christian faith. The moment that the other two dimensions (the reflective and the affective dimensions) are excluded, you end up with **activism**. The same holds true for the blue segment. As essential as the affective dimension is, if our focus is exclusively reduced to it, we will end up in **emotionalism**, which has already done much damage to the church.

Strengthening the opposite pole

How can we best overcome these dangers? One option is to warn and even to fight against each of them. That's possible, and sometimes even necessary. However, another option would be to strengthen the "balancing" poles. Do you want

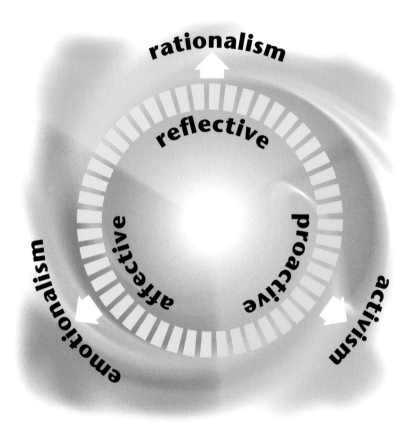

As long as there is an equilibrium of the reflective, pro-active, and affective dimensions, the church organism is healthy. If one of the three colors is neglected, we run into the dangers of rationalism, activism, and emotionalism.

to overcome rationalism? Then strengthen the proactive and affective sides. Do you want to tackle activism? Strengthen the reflective and the affective sides. Do you want to fight emotionalism? Strengthen the reflective and the proactive sides. Isn't the pursuit of radical balance healthier than pursuing conflict?

This way of dealing with things is unfamiliar to many people, especially within Western cultures. In some non-Western cultures, however, especially in the East, it's the most natural thing in the world—for example, tackling a disease by strengthening the balancing pole of the body. Inter-cultural learning can enable us to find new, creative, and spiritual ways of conflict management.

Dealing with our own danger zones

It's amazing how many of us clearly see the heresies of other Christian groups, but are relatively blind toward our own. Let's assume your own group tends to rationalism. Then you don't need to warn your people against emotionalism and activism—since that's not your problem—but rather, address your personal danger zone: rationalism.

Which of the three areas is your primary danger zone?

Chapter 2

What you can learn from green churches

All of the strengths of green churches are related to the fact that they have understood in a profound way that God is the Creator. This fundamental insight has shaped their view of Jesus and the Holy Spirit as well. When some representatives of the green zone speak about Jesus or the Spirit, it's often just a variation of what they share about God the Creator.

Taking responsibility for all of God's creation is one of the strengths of green churches.

Since God is the Creator not only of Christians, but of all human beings—they may be Muslims, Buddhists, materialists, or agnostics—churches with a green focus are able to see what they have in common with other religious or non-religious people. Because of that fact, green churches display a high degree of tolerance. They don't tend toward fundamentalism. They like to combine efforts with non-Christians when it comes to accomplishing tasks that are focused on serving God's creation.

The reflective tendency

Usually, green churches have a high view of intellectual reflection. Social and natural sciences are not seen as something that is in competition with the Christian faith, but as an integral part of a Christian world view. You don't have to invest a lot of energy to convince a representative of this color zone that conducting empirical research in the church can be of spiritual significance. They already know it.

Their emphasis on God's creation manifests itself in an openness to the arts. Sensual ways of experiencing the divine reality are usually given priority over puritanical, non-experiential forms. Dance, drama, and music may play an important role in churches of the other color zones as well; for green churches, however, the arts are far more than just "tools" to communicate a spiritual message. They have a spiritual significance in their own right as reflections of God's creativity. This view of creation strongly shapes their worship services. They usually display a more artistic liturgy than we find in churches of the other color zones.

The focus on society

Green churches don't view issues such as protecting the environment or social justice just as "means to evangelize," like churches of the other color zones tend to do. They regard these activities as biblical mandates. When it comes to fundamental change processes in society (overcoming dictatorships, fighting racism, working for reconciliation, etc.), very often green churches play a significant role. Many representatives of these churches are involved in politics and the media.

My experiences:

According to our research, the most frequent minimum factors of liberal churches are passionate spirituality and need-oriented evangelism, while their greatest strength is empowering leadership. When ministering in groups with this starting point, I try to help them experience growth both in the red and the blue zones. Usually I can sense how eager they are to improve in those areas, as long as they don't have to adopt a style that doesn't fit them. Therefore, I stress that growing in the red zone doesn't mean adopting an "evangelical style," but emphasizing biblical standards, including the Great Commission. Likewise, growing in the blue zone doesn't imply imitating the style of charismatic churches, but it does mean experiencing more spiritual power.

*Green churches stress the **reflective** dimension more than the affective and proactive dimensions. In their ministry, they focus on **tolerance** and **social justice**. Their agenda gives topics like **science**, **art**, and **politics** a prominent place.*

The limitations

All of these aspects are strengths that churches of the other color zones would benefit from. If we are looking for the dangers of green churches, we shouldn't make the mistake of criticizing them for their strengths, but rather for their relative neglect of the other two color zones.

The more the red and the blue colors are ignored, the more likely relativistic and syncretistic tendencies will emerge. There are green churches that not only abstain from all forms of evangelistic outreach (red zone), but also argue why it is important not to evangelize. And some not only display a poorly developed blue zone, but try to make us believe that this weakness is in fact a sign of intellectual maturity or aesthetic superiority.

However, the majority of green churches that I have encountered in the context of the NCD ministry are different. They are able to see their strengths, but they recognize their limitations. While they don't have any reason to leave their area of strength, they are eager to mature by moving deeper into the other color zones.

Which aspects of green churches would help you to mature as a Christian?

Chapter 2

What you can learn from red churches

R egardless of denominational or cultural differences, churches that are primarily strong in the red zone have a lot of things in common. They place the cross of Jesus at the very center, not just as a religious symbol, but as a point of orientation for all of their activities. The sacrificial dimension of the Christian faith plays a more important role for them than for representatives of the other two color zones.

Churches of the red zone rightly place the cross of Jesus at the center of all they do.

When red churches speak about the Creator or the Holy Spirit, it's basically just a variation of their message about Christ. They strongly emphasize the absolute claims of Jesus. Scripture is the normative standard for all they do. They can be very strong when it comes to resisting the "spirit of the times." Compromising biblical standards is not an option for them.

The proactive tendency

Of course, churches of the other two color zones can be quite active as well. But for red churches the proactive tendency is more prominent than it is for the others. They don't ask primarily, "Is it fun?", "Does it feel good?", or, "Does it work?" Rather they ask, "Is this God's will?" Red churches have, on average, a better developed sense of duty than churches of the other color zones.

My experiences:

When selecting all non-charismatic evangelical churches in our data bank, we discovered that their most frequent minimum factor is loving relationships. This certainly corresponds to a widespread cliché about evangelicals: They are good in doctrine, but not so good in practicing love. Legalistic tendencies, in particular, have a strong negative bearing on loving relationships. More surprising is the greatest strength of "red" churches, which turned out to be gift-based ministry, a characteristic that, according to another widespread cliché, is owned by charismatics. However, it can be demonstrated that, on average, non-charismatics rank higher when it comes to applying gifts to specific tasks in the church. Empirical reality can differ remarkably from theological stereotypes.

This tendency strongly shapes their spirituality. In most red churches, discipleship plays a prominent role, and the activities in this area reveal that the term is related to "discipline." Their focus is on personal ethics. Representatives of red churches may get involved in politics, just as members of green churches do. But if they do, their passion is very likely to be focused on "micro ethics," such as marriage and family, rather than "macro ethics," such as ecology or economic justice.

The focus on evangelism

Red churches can be seen as advocates of the "salvation revelation," since they rightly emphasize the necessity of a personal relationship to Christ. Therefore, the topic of evangelism is of utmost importance to them. People who are lost without Christ need to be saved. Red churches strive to involve as many people as possible in personal evangelism, which is frequently the focal point of their discipleship training.

Some of them may develop a number of activities that appear "green" or "blue" from the outside, but a closer look reveals that the green or blue color shadings are primarily means to the end of getting people interested in the gospel. The real focus is that people get to know Christ personally; the other aspects are not unimportant, but they are secondary.

*Red churches stress the **proactive** dimension more than the affective and reflective dimensions. In their ministry, they focus on **evangelism** and **discipleship**. Their agenda gives topics like **Scripture**, **devotions**, and **personal ethics** a prominent place.*

The limitations

The strengths that red churches display should not be seen as just their personal "hobby horses." Red churches focus on the very topics without which the church would cease to exist. Their weakness is not their stress of the color red, but their relative neglect of the other two color zones.

What are the consequences if both the green and the blue areas are underdeveloped? The absolute claims of Jesus, the normative standards of Scripture, and the need to evangelize the world still remain, but without pursuing balance in the green and blue color segments, red churches are in danger of becoming legalistic. We should never forget that legalism, according to the New Testament, is a serious problem. It's a heresy just as syncretism is. Some red churches develop a notion of "self righteousness" that makes them immune to seeing any need for change.

But again, the majority of red churches that I have encountered in the context of the NCD ministry is different. They are eager to learn from the other color segments, as they sense that this is necessary to fulfill their calling: winning the world for Christ. They are well aware that they have a lot to give, but also that there is still a lot to learn. Again, radical balance.

Which aspects of red churches would help you to mature as a Christian?

What we can learn from blue churches

Spiritual power and emotional health are strengths of blue churches.

My experiences:

According to our research in 40,000 churches worldwide, guess what was the most frequent minimum factor in charismatic churches? Gift-based ministry, surprisingly enough. There are, of course, countless charismatic churches that have their greatest strength in that area, but on average it is just the other way around. A closer look shows that this remarkable discovery is not too difficult to explain. The weaker the green and red segments are, the more difficult it will be to implement a gift-based approach for the whole church in a systematic and consistent way. The greatest strength of charismatic churches isn't difficult to guess. It is passionate spirituality. That is the natural fruit of being involved so much in the blue zone.

When we talk about "blue churches," we have to keep in mind that the majority of charismatic and pentecostal churches are actually "red/blue" churches. At least among protestant churches, they are as much evangelical as they are charismatic, but they sometimes show markedly "anti-green" tendencies.

Blue churches can be seen as advocates of God's revelation in the Holy Spirit. For them it is essential that the Holy Spirit is not just accepted at an intellectual level, but that people experience him as a life-changing reality. It's certainly not true that red and green churches have completely excluded the Holy Spirit, but for blue churches he plays a far more prominent role. Without experiencing the supernatural power of the Spirit, blue churches would miss something that is part of the essence of the church.

The affective tendency

Whereas many churches of the other color zones view the topic of "spiritual experiences" with a certain amount of skepticism, for blue churches it's definitely a positive term. Their focus is not so much on the head (as in green churches), or on the hands (as in red churches), but on the heart.

This elevated view of the affective side of Christianity permeates all aspects of ministry. Themes such as "inner healing" and "restored emotions" are more likely to be found in blue churches than in churches of the other color zones. Even when blue churches approach topics such as "forgiveness" (a classical red theme) or "reconciliation" (a green theme), the affective side plays the dominant role. The same can be observed in the practice of worship. In many cases, people are strongly encouraged to express their emotions publicly.

The focus on spiritual power

The driving force behind blue churches is their quest for spiritual power. Expecting "signs and wonders" often plays an important role. This focus also explains why in these churches some of the gifts mentioned in the New Testament (such as prophesy, healing, or tongues) are given more attention than other New Testament gifts (such as organization, teaching, or service).

It should be noticed that a strong blue zone is not restricted to churches within the charismatic movement. There are countless churches outside of the charismatic family that have a strong focus on the experiential side of faith and on spiritual power. In many cases, these groups are more introverted and mystical in orientation than a classic Pentecostal would be.

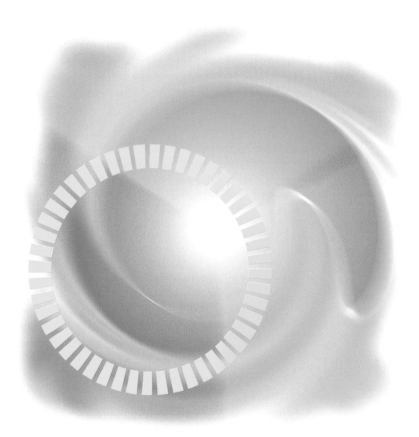

*Blue churches stress the **affective** dimension more than the reflective and proactive dimensions. In their ministry, they focus on **spiritual power** and **emotional health**. Their agenda gives topics like **worship**, **signs and wonders**, and **spiritual experiences** a prominent place.*

The limitations

People who criticize blue churches for their strengths are in danger of criticizing the possibility of personally experiencing the living God. Churches of all color segments should seek to incorporate more of this dimension into their own ministries. However, to the degree that a blue church neglects the other two color segments, it is in danger of creating more problems than it solves.

Churches with an underdeveloped red zone run the risk of placing more authority on inner pictures, personal impressions, and dreams than on Scripture. A neglect of the green zone is equally dangerous. It results in only seeing those things that are in contrast to God's creational order as "truly spiritual." In extreme cases, this can lead to a fully escapist lifestyle.

Thankfully, there are very few *pure* blue churches, just as *purely* green and red churches are the exception, not the rule. In most churches, we can find all three colors. It's just that one of them is more strongly developed than the others. A blue church like that will usually be eager to experience more of "God's fullness" in the green and red zones.

Which aspects of blue churches would help you to mature as a Christian?

Five rules of the Trinitarian Compass

Take a look at the picture on the right. Throughout this book, you will encounter this image several times, as its message communicates what the Trinitarian Compass is all about. When I do NCD conferences, I like to ask the participants the following question, "Do the figures in this picture move in the same direction, or in different directions?"

Different directions—or the same direction?

Normally, about 50% answer, "Different directions," while the other 50% opt for, "The same direction." From a linear point of view only one of the two answers can be right, but within the logic of the Trinitarian Compass, both answers are correct at the same time. In fact, all of the figures move in the same direction, which is toward the center. But depending on their individual starting points, they have to take different, sometimes even opposite, directions to get there.

> We have to train people to view the world from the perspective of the three color zones.

In the context of this picture, these dynamics are quite easy to grasp. And at the moment we have understood them we have understood highly complex dynamics of theology and church life. We have also understood how the Trinitarian Compass functions: People move in different directions, and yet all of them move in the same direction, which is closer to the living God.

The metaphor of the compass

For that reason, I have chosen the metaphor of a "compass." Used in conjunction with a map, a compass helps you to (a) locate where you are at the moment, and (b) help you get to your destination. However, it doesn't provide you with a step-by-step plan for how to get there. If there are three people who have to approach a certain destination from different starting points, the same sort of compass will show them extremely different directions for getting there.

More on the web:

On the internet (see page 162) you will find answers to the following questions:

- *Is "balance" really a growth factor? Many growing churches seem to be rather one-sided.*

- *How does the Roman-Catholic Church fit into the color scheme?*

Rule 1: Apply the Trinitarian Compass to different areas and levels of church life

You will encounter the Trinitarian Compass in many different contexts within NCD. It will always identify your starting point *related to a specific subject.* You might discover, for instance, that in the area of need-oriented evangelism you are very "green," while in the area of gift-based ministry, you are predominantly "red," and in the area of loving relationships, "blue/green." It would be misleading to assume that, once you have identified a certain color tendency, the same color applies to all areas of your life. The colors can be different depending on the subject under consideration.

One of the most beneficial ways of using the Trinitarian Compass is to apply it to different levels of church life: individual believers, small

Are these figures moving in the same direction or in different directions? Within the Trinitarian Compass, both answers are simultaneously correct. All figures move in the same direction, i.e. toward the center. But depending on their starting points, they have to move in different, even opposite, directions in order reach that destination.

groups, entire churches, and denominations. Comparing these results with each other can be extremely eye-opening. Just consider the relationship between your personal results and those of your church!

Rule 2: Accept that every believer is out of balance

All of the biblical characters (whether it be Moses, David, Mary, or Paul), all of the heroes of church history (whether it be Augustine, Luther, Moody, or Mother Teresa), and all of our contemporary Christian heroes have been out of balance. The only exception to this rule—really, the only one—is Jesus, the Son of God.

I am out of balance, and you are out of balance. Your pastor is out of balance, and your bishop (if you have one) is out of balance. Regretfully, there are a number of Christian biographies that portray their specific heroes as perfectly balanced people. As long as it is not a biography about Jesus, you can be sure that such a portrait is historically inaccurate. Human beings are not like that. This realization enables us to speak openly, even publicly, about "color deficiencies," as all of us have areas of weakness and strength.

Rule 3: Be alert to the specific danger that is connected to every color

In this book, we have repeatedly dealt with the fact that every color is related to a specific danger. The less developed the other two colors, the more likely that danger will occur. Always remember that heresy is usually not the opposite of the truth, but a partial truth. Don't confuse the Trinitarian Compass with an activity designed for spiritual entertainment.

When one considers the dangers that can be encountered in all three directions, we are speaking about a very serious subject.

> We have to minister to people on the basis of their starting points, not ours.

My experiences:

When I am invited to liberal groups (green zone), I love to share about how I found Christ (red) and how I have experienced the power of the Holy Spirit (blue). I don't do that in evangelical (red) or charismatic groups (blue). There I focus, for instance, on the area of social justice (green). This is my way of "focusing on the opposing pole." I know that this is the very opposite of how things "normally" function. I hope, however, that the procedure that I try to model will become more normal in the future, as it is more healthy and productive than the established patterns.

> *Which of these rules presents the greatest contrast to your past experience?*

Rule 4: Always focus on the opposing pole of your current strength

On pages 58-59, we have already dealt with the concept of the "opposing pole." The challenge, however, is not just to agree to the idea, but to actually apply it to your life. The wonderful thing about this concept is that it enables you to tackle even serious dangers, such as heresies, in a positive way.

Let's assume the current strength of your church is in the affective area (blue) and its danger zone is emotionalism. Focusing on the "opposing pole" (which would be the green and red zones with their focus on reflection and proactivity), will automatically protect you from your danger zone. You don't have to preach sermons about the dangers of emotionalism and why it leads people directly to hell. Simply preaching about how to grow in the opposite color areas will achieve your goal far more effectively. It is amazing how well this concept works, regardless of what your starting point is and how severely your danger zone may manifest itself.

Rule 5: Minister to other people on the basis of their starting points, not yours

You have probably experienced the following: Your pastor has been to a conference and made a wonderful spiritual discovery. From that day on everyone at your church has to make exactly the same discovery. Or you have discovered that strengthening your reflective side is the next step in your Christian pilgrimage, and now you make the unfortunate people around you believe that this is also the most important step for them. Or your small group leader has read a book that has helped her tackle a crucial area of her life. Now she is having all of the small group members read that book and deal with the same "crucial issue." From a human point of view, such reactions are understandable, but they are incredibly immature. At the very least, Christian leaders should not allow themselves to act like that.

Frequently, especially at Christian conferences, I have heard appeals that follow one of these schemes: "All of us have to...", "What everybody needs is...", "The core problem in our lives is...", or "The key for your life is..." Whenever I hear this, I am relatively sure that these speakers, while making helpful suggestions for about one third of the audience, lead the other two thirds in the wrong direction. Since everyone has a different starting point, everyone needs different guidance.

The Trinitarian Compass and the doctrine of the Trinity

How does the Trinitarian Compass relate to the doctrine of the Trinity? In the fourth century, the church had to tackle the question of how speaking about the Father, the Son, and the Holy Spirit relates to the belief that there is only one God. From these discussions arose the classical doctrine of the Trinity, which has been taught to this day: God is understood as "one substance" *(una substantia)* and "three persons" *(tres personae).*

When dealing with the Trinitarian Compass (see diagram on page 53), we have used different terms and categories than the ones mentioned above: the metaphor of light; the three colors; the focus on change processes and spiritual growth; the context of church development; the terms "Creator," "Jesus," and "Spirit" around the term "God" in the center. The question arises: Is this the same doctrine, or is it different from the classical doctrine?

Two different questions

The Trinitarian Compass is rooted in the classical formula of the fourth century. However, what many people don't realize is that each paradigm deals with a different question:

1. The focus of the classical doctrine is on the question of how the **three persons of the Godhead** relate to each other.

2. The Trinitarian Compass focuses on the question of how **we (the believers)** relate to the triune God.

Both questions are important, but they are *not* the same. Thus it can be confusing to use the same conceptual tools that have been developed to address the first topic in order to understand the essence of the second topic, or vice versa. Every paradigm has been developed to address one specific issue, and the same paradigm that answers one question well does not necessarily provide answers to the other questions, as it was never designed for that purpose.

What is our focus?

Just as the classical doctrine doesn't answer the question of how we, as individual believers and whole churches, relate to the triune God, the Trinitarian Compass doesn't answer the question of how to define the interrelationship of the persons of the Godhead. Sometimes people firmly believe that I have addressed the question of their interrelationship in my books, when in reality I haven't said a single word about this theme—not because I deem it unimportant, but in the context of the NCD paradigm, it is not my topic.

The Trinitarian Compass is an attempt to relate the doctrine of the Trinity to life.

More on the web:

On the internet (see page 162) you will find answers to the following questions:

• *How biblical is Natural Church Development?*

• *Doesn't the Trinitarian Compass show a tendency to what throughout church history has been called "modalism"?*

Is the Trinitarian Compass orthodox?

The times when the three dimensions were interrelated, were the best times of the church.

My experiences:

In many discussions about the Trinitarian Compass I have observed an interesting pattern. In our theological training, we learn specific paradigms (such as Greek metaphysics), terms (such as monarchism, modalism, dynamism), names of authors (like Sabellius), etc. When we later encounter concepts in newer writings (say, in an NCD book), we tend to interpret those concepts using the information that we have acquired from other books, making the assumption that both authors are trying to present the same line of thought. One might recall, for instance, that a specific heretic had used the light metaphor, as we do in the Trinitarian Compass. As a result, they project the misguided teaching of this heretic on NCD, accusing us of statements that we neither teach nor share.

However, when people don't take this difference into consideration, they get confused by the fact that the Trinitarian Compass uses "different" categories than the classical doctrine. They ask me questions like these:

• Why do you *substitute* the term "Father" with "Creator" or "Son" with "Jesus"?

• Why, in your diagram, do you *add* a fourth element, namely the term "God" at the very center?

• Why do you *refuse* to use the term "persons"?

In reality, I haven't substituted anything; I haven't added anything; and I haven't refused anything. This impression can only arise when people operate under the assumption that both paradigms address the same question, and that I have taken the classical formulations and changed them to fit my purposes. However, nothing like that has happened.

No competition between the two paradigms

The fact that the Trinitarian Compass uses different terms and categories than the classical formulations, has the same background as the fact that different Bible verses use different formulations to address different, but related, topics. If in one reference Jesus is called the "Son of God," and in another, "the Lamb," it would be absurd to conclude that the term "Son of God" had been *substituted* with the term "Lamb." It is just another way of describing a specific aspect of Jesus in a specific context.

There are many instances in Scripture in which Jesus is not referred to as "the Son," but simply as "Jesus." If I use the term "Jesus" in our paradigm, that is no more heretical than the biblical use of that term would be. The same applies to the use of the terms "Father," "Spirit," "Creator," etc. When it comes to speaking about God, Scripture offers us a plethora of terms, titles, and names.

Relating the doctrine to life

The Trinitarian Compass is an attempt to relate the doctrine of the Trinity to life. It deliberately places the Trinity in the context of personal growth and church development. It seeks to build a bridge between the theological question about the nature of God, and the empirical question about change processes in a local church.

In the past, people have repeatedly asked me if I "affirmed" the doctrine of the Trinity, as they obviously had the impres-

What distinguishes Christianity from all other religions is God's threefold revelation: His revelation in creation (green zone), symbolized by the rainbow; his revelation in Jesus Christ (red zone), symbolized by the cross; and his revelation in the Holy Spirit (blue zone), symbolized by the dove.

sion that I would have difficulty with that. Whenever I receive such a request, my answer is, "I see the core of our ministry as helping bring to life what the fathers of that doctrine fought for. In my mind, that is taking a doctrine far more seriously than pure verbal affirmation would be."

It's a tragedy that the doctrine of the Trinity is regarded, by and large, as a lifeless, irrelevant concept that, though theologically central, has nothing to do with our daily lives. My heart rejoices when I see that this is changing dramatically, and that the NCD Community is an important part of this global movement.

How to avoid dangers

The doctrine of the Trinity was not developed to be an end in itself, but primarily to defend the Christian faith against clearly definable dangers. Church history has shown that it is not possible to defend the truth merely by the formulation of orthodox creeds. The truth only becomes manifest when people holistically experience who the trinitarian God is, with their heads, their hands, and their hearts. That is what we are committed to achieve in Natural Church Development.

In the past, has the doctrine of the Trinity played any practical role in your life?

The NCD Color Profile

Chapter 2

The NCD Color Profile will reveal which of the three colors is currently most strongly developed in your own life, and which one should be your primary area of focus. If you are studying this book together with other church members, the Color Profile can be evaluated for your whole church as well.

This test is not for spiritual entertainment, but should be part of a developmental process.

My experiences:

Again and again, people have asked me why they can't get copies of the Color Profile or other NCD-related surveys as a "separate test" rather than as part of a book. The main reason why we have decided not to design separate tests is that we don't want to foster a "fast food mentality" that would use these kinds of tools more for spiritual entertainment than as an integral part of a serious developmental process. Outside the context of this book and apart from the explanations given to the readers, this test doesn't make any sense. It could even be counterproductive, as the pure "results" would create more misunderstandings than answers.

Before you begin the test, a few words of explanation:

1 Read through the following 36 statements and place an "x" in the column that best describes you or your church. Answer as spontaneously as possible, and be honest with yourself. Note that questions 1-18 deal with your own life and questions 19-36, with the life of your church. You may wish to use a pencil to fill in the questionnaire so that you can repeat the test at a later date.

2 When you have answered all of the questions, follow the instructions on page 75. You will be able to calculate *your personal results* immediately.

3 In order to obtain *your church's results,* give page 75 to the person administering the survey. He or she will add your answers to that of the other members of your church and receive the results once all of the data has been collected and uploaded to the NCD web site.

*If you are the **pastor** or person responsible for administering this profile, please do the following:*

1 Be sure that you don't use the Color Profile just for entertainment, but try to integrate it into a structured developmental process. Make sure that each participant in this process has a copy of this book. Note that there are large discounts available for the use of the book as a whole church. For more information, contact the publisher (the contact address is provided on page 2).

2 To get results for your church, at least 30% of your regular worshipping congregation should have a copy of this book and fill out the questionnaire.

3 Please collect the completed page 75 from each participant and enter the data in the spreadsheet that can be found at *www.ncd-international.org/community.* Once you have uploaded the data, you will immediately get the results for your church. They will be calculated based on a statistical norm that has been developed for your country and language.

The evaluation through the internet is free of charge. It is an exclusive service for readers of *Color Your World with Natural Church Development.*

The following statement applies to me:

	very much	to a large extent	moderately	slightly	not at all	
1						It's important for me to invest a lot of time in reflective thinking.
2						If something needs to be done, I want to be involved.
3						It's important to me to feel God's presence in my life.
4						I enjoy being around people whose lifestyle is different than mine.
5						My life is focused on helping other people find a personal relationship with Christ.
6						It's important for me to feel uplifted when meeting God in prayer.
7						Social justice plays an important role in my everyday decisions.
8						It's important for me to practice disciplines that strengthen my commitment to Christ.
9						The Holy Spirit leads me in my daily decisions.
10						I am actively involved in political issues.
11						Reading the Bible daily is important to me.
12						I have often experienced supernatural manifestations of God's power.
13						I try to expose myself to the arts on a regular basis.
14						Time set aside for spiritual contemplation is an integral part of my life.
15						I am significantly uplifted through times of praise and worship.
16						I base my decisions on scientific data.
17						For me, the center of Christian ethics is personal holiness.
18						I frequently sense God's presence in my life.
	4	3	2	1	0	

The following statement applies to my church:

	very much	to a large extent	moderately	slightly	not at all	
19						The climate of our church is predominantly intellectual.
20						Our church motivates people to be involved in ministry.
21						Our church does its best to create a warm atmosphere.
22						Differing opinions are valued in our church.
23						Our church actively supports its members in their evangelistic activities.
24						Many of our church activities are geared toward helping members restore their emotional lives.
25						Our church actively pursues social justice.
26						Our church actively supports believers as they grow in their relationship to Christ.
27						In our church's activities, we frequently experience manifestations of the power of the Holy Spirit.
28						Our church stresses the political implications of Christianity.
29						The authority of the Bible plays an important role in the life of our church.
30						Expecting signs and wonders is an important characteristic of our church.
31						Our church reflects a high view of the arts.
32						Devotional times are a normal part of many church meetings.
33						Praise and worship times are central to our church's make-up.
34						Scientific reasoning plays an important role in the life of our church.
35						In spite of the spirit of the times, our church is known for resisting moral compromise.
36						Our church has a high view of spiritual experience.
	4	3	2	1	0	

How to evaluate the NCD Color Profile

Chapter 2

Have you answered all of the questions? Then you can begin with the evaluation. It is quite simple if you follow the seven steps explained below:

Step 1: Tear out this page

Remove the evaluation sheet by tearing along the perforation.

Step 2: Collect the raw data

Using the following two scoring grids (Table A and Table B), enter the numbers that correspond to your answers on the questionnaire. These numbers can be found at the bottom of each answer column (4-0).

Table A

						Color	Total
1	4	7	10	13	16	Green	
2	5	8	11	14	17	Red	
3	6	9	12	15	18	Blue	

Table B

						Color
19	22	25	28	31	34	Green
20	23	26	29	32	35	Red
21	24	27	30	33	36	Blue

Step 3: Add up the data in Table A

Now add up the six numbers in every row of Table A. Write the result for each row in the *Total* field. This will give you a "raw value" for each color. You don't have to add up the figures for Table B.

Note that the *Totals* of Table A do not represent the results of your personal Color Profile. To get your personal results, you will need to transfer the raw data (calculated above) into the "normation table" found on page 76.

The scientific normation has been developed by the Institute for Natural Church Development on the basis of inter-denominational sample groups and is different for every language edition of this book.

Continue on the next page.

How to evaluate the NCD Color Profile (continued)

Step 4: Transfer the raw data to the normation table

Transfer the totals for each color of Table A onto the normation table on the right. Circle the number yielded on the scoring grid for each color. For example, if the scoring grid shows a total of 19 for *Red,* you should circle the number 19 in the normation table for the row labeled *Red.* If the corresponding number does not appear, simply circle the next lowest number.

Step 5: View your personal results

The normation table now shows you which color has the highest value, and which one the lowest (see *profile values* in the black row). This will give you an indication of which areas you should focus on. Write the profile values for each of the three colors into the table on page 77, *Your Personal Color Profile.*

> The Color Profile will give you an indication of which areas you should focus on.

Step 6: Evaluate your church's Color Profile

In order to get the Color Profile for your whole church, follow these steps:

a. Hand this page of the book to the person who is responsible for administering the survey in your church. He or she will need both the results of Table A and Table B, since both will be used for calculating your church's results.

b. Once your church has the data of at least 30% of your worshipping congregation, the person responsible for administering the survey can upload all of the data to the internet. He or she will immediately receive your church's NCD Color Profile that is based on a statistical norm that has been developed for churches in your country.

c. Contact this person to get the final results of your church's Color Profile. Write them into the table on page 77, *Your Church's Color Profile.*

Step 7: Continue with chapter 6

Note that chapter 6 (starting on page 166) explicitly deals with the question of how to proceed once you have identified the Color Profiles both for yourself and for your church. If you are very experienced with NCD, you can continue on from page 166.

Normation table (raw score 20 → 80):

Raw	20	21	22	23	24	25	26	27	28	29	30	31	32	33	34	35	36	37	38	39	40	41	42	43	44	45	46	47	48	49	50	51	52	53	54	55	56	57	58	59	60	61	62	63	64	65	66	67	68	69	70	71	72	73	74	75	76	77	78	79	80
Profile values	0				1		2			3		4			5			6		7			8		9			10			11			12			13			14			15			16			17			18			19			20		21		22
Green	0			1			2		3		4		5			6		7			8		9			10			11			12			13		14			15		16			17			18			19			20					21			22
Red	0			1			2		3			4		5			6		7		8		9			10			11		12			13		14		15			16		17		18		19			20		21		22			23		24
Blue	0			1			2			3		4		5			6		7		8		9			10		11		12		13		14		15			16		17			18		19		20			21			22		23		24

Your spiritual roadmap

I t is one thing to identify your starting point (which has been the purpose of the preceding few pages), and it is a different thing to develop your personal spiritual roadmap (which is the focus of the remaining pages of this book). To be realistic, I recognize that the majority of those who complete the Color Profile will never do anything practical with the results. There is a widespread tendency, especially in the Western world, to use these kinds of instruments just for "self-discovery," rather than seeing them as the starting point of a long-term growth process.

I want to invite you, however, to enter a process of personal transformation. If you have the opportunity to participate in this process together with fellow believers—or even with your whole church—so much the better. I don't know your personal starting point and your specific problem areas, but what I do know is that this process will lead you to an increasingly higher level of maturity. Guaranteed!

Your results

Before you continue, please write down the three "profile values" revealed in your personal Color Profile. You can find the "profile values" in the black bar of the normation table on page 76:

Your Personal Color Profile
Your Profile Value for Green: _____
Your Profile Value for Red: _____
Your Profile Value for Blue: _____

On the following table, you can write down the "profile values" for your church as a whole. You will need to get these values from the person who was responsible for administering the survey in your church.

Your Church's Color Profile
Your Church's Profile Value for Green: _____
Your Church's Profile Value for Red: _____
Your Church's Profile Value for Blue: _____

The Trinitarian Compass will lead you to an increasingly higher level of maturity.

My experiences:

I love to utilize this and other "Three-Color Tests" in the context of NCD conferences, as they help relate the abstract teaching on the three colors immediately to our own lives. This works especially well if radical representatives of the three colors are present. When I invite the participants to work in small groups (each of them encompassing different colors) most of them experience how beneficial it is to network with people who are strong in those color zones that are weakly developed in their own lives. There is no other part of an NCD conference in which I have observed so much laughter, so many tears, and such intense prayer, as in the course of these exercises.

Your personal Color Profile

*Use the diagram at the right to display your **personal** Color Profile. Take the "profile values" from the table "Your Personal Color Profile" on page 77. Place an "X" on each of the three dotted lines at the location that corresponds most closely to your numbers. Connect the three points to make a triangle. The picture below shows you how the image may look in the end.*

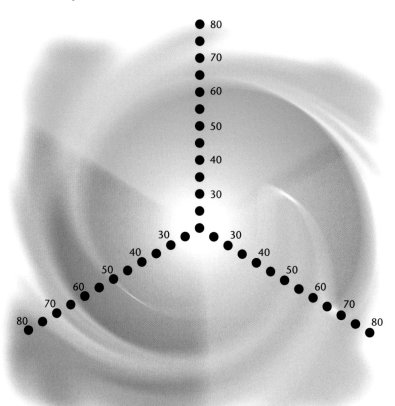

Develop a graphical representation

Sample of a graphical representation of the NCD Color Profile.

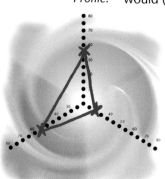

You may find it helpful to develop a graphical representation of the two Color Profiles. If you follow the instructions above, your results will be displayed in the form of a triangle. For most people, such a picture communicates far better than the three numbers in and of themselves would (see sample to the left).

This graphical representation will reveal that usually none of the colors is completely absent, and none is perfectly represented. It's more a question of *how strongly* each of the colors is represented. If you should find out that you have a relatively balanced Color Profile, don't take this as an indication that you have already reached your goal. Work toward growth in all three color areas.

Results change over time

Please keep in mind that the current Color Profile only describes your present situation. If you or your church should repeat the profile at a later date, you might get different

Your church's Color Profile

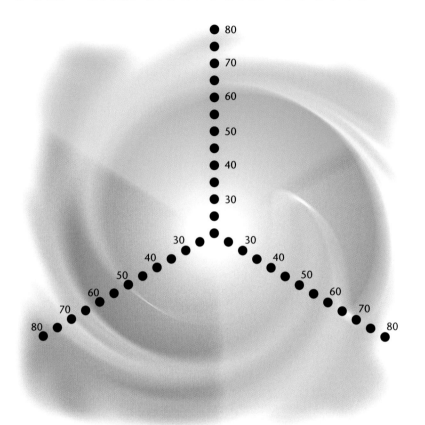

*Use the diagram at the left to display your **church's** Color Profile. Ask the person responsible for administering the profile to give you the corporate results for the green, red, and blue areas of your church. As with your personal profile, connect the three points to make a triangle.*

results, especially if you decide to specifically focus on one of the color areas in the intervening time period. By repeating the profile you can determine whether or not you have made progress in your development process.

Compass and roadmap

How can you practically develop a roadmap both for yourself and for your church? Chapter 6 of this book deals with this question. If you are already familiar with the NCD principles, you might wish to skip to that chapter. However, chapters 3-5 will give you a better understanding of what the individual NCD principles are all about and what tools are available to implement them into the life of your church.

If you should use the Color Profile in the context of an NCD Campaign (see page 164), the results will play an important role throughout the process. You will get a number of additional tools to interpret the results of the Color Profile on an individual and corporate level. Moreover, you will experience what it means in practical terms for a large number of believers to be involved in such a process simultaneously. Enjoy!

In light of the Color Profile, what would be the most important next step for you?

The
Principles

3

Human growth principles can bring about results: success in business, economic improvement, even church growth. However, the problem with many of these human concepts is that there is no inherent sustainable power behind them. They depend on great amounts of outside energy, and once that energy is reduced, everything collapses. What a contrast to the dynamics that we observe in God's creation, where the following principle is at work: Remove the barriers and growth takes place "all by itself." It is not a human responsibility to energize the church. God takes care of that.

Principles—the inflation of a term

O ver the past few years, it has become fashionable to talk about principles. I am not sure whether I should rejoice in that or not. Sure, in contrast to ten years ago we can observe a new concern about the deeper roots of spiritual fruit. That is a positive development.

> ## Principles focus on the source, not on the outer manifestations.

My experiences:

Recently I spoke to a representative of a famous model church. "The way you position NCD as a principle-oriented approach against church models is not helpful," he said. "Model churches, such as ours, teach principles as much as you do." It's certainly correct that the majority of model churches talk a lot about principles. But what many people fail to see is that within a model-oriented mindset the term "principle" means something different than it does in NCD. In many cases, the foundational features of a specific model are simply referred to as "principles," whether they apply to all cultures, all church sizes, and all spiritual styles or not. In most cases, there is no truly global evidence that can verify whether or not those criteria are fulfilled.

However, since the frequent use of the term "principle" has resulted in an inflation of the term, there is hardly any feature of church life that hasn't been presented as a "principle." Whether people are speaking about spiritual warfare, a seeker-sensitive worship service, a specific way of organizing small groups, or a certain pattern of evangelistic outreach, the term "principle" can be found everywhere. This use of the term has contributed to considerable confusion.

Why we need a clear definition of the term

For that reason, I have listed the criteria that we apply in NCD when we use this term (see page 19). We only speak about a principle of church development when we refer to a feature that (a) is universally valid, (b) has been proven by research, (c) is focused on the essentials of the church, and (d) needs to be individualized in different situations.

My plea for a clear definition of the term "principle" is not so much driven by purely academic considerations, but by practical concerns. If someone tries to sell you a certain feature of church life as a "principle" without giving you empirical proof that it is universally applicable, you simply cannot know whether it will work in your situation. Perhaps it will, perhaps it won't.

If you are dealing with a true principle, however, you know from the outset that it will work. Your challenge is to *contextualize* the principle to your own particular situation (our criteria d). This process of contextualizing universal principles to local contexts is what Natural Church Development is all about.

Why research is important

Many Christians don't yet understand why our institute has focused on empirical studies for so many years, since "research" is not often regarded as a discipline of high spiritual significance. The reason for our one-sided focus is easy to explain. We wanted to teach universal principles, not just "helpful ideas." And without universal research there is no way to know whether or not you are dealing with a truly universal principle of church development.

Many of the things that we were able to identify as "principles" were right in line with what people might have expected and with what the majority of church growth textbooks had

Since universal principles, by definition, apply to all sorts of cultural settings, there is a unifying power behind the principle-oriented approach.

always taught. There were other features, however, that came as a surprise to us all. Many of the things that I teach today I used to teach very differently before we completed our research. The ongoing challenge of a scientific approach is to adapt a theory to empirical evidence, which enables constant improvement.

Universal principles and personal values

Since principles, by definition, apply to any situation, they also apply to all sorts of church models. It can be demonstrated that every model church is only successful to the degree that it applies, whether consciously or unconsciously, those principles that we have chosen to call Natural Church Development. This discovery is one of the most revealing aspects of our research in 40,000 churches. For this reason, following a specific church model should never be seen as something that is in competition with following NCD's principle-oriented approach. No model church can do without the principles that are described in this book.

An increasing number of churches that follow a specific model have purposely decided to implement the principles of NCD as part of their daily routine. Thus they implement both universal principles of church health and distinctives of the model of their choice. While the *principles* reflect what they have in common with all healthy churches around the globe, the specifics of the model are what distinguishes them from other churches. These are expressions of their *values*; indicators of what they have discovered to be valuable to them. I think that this is a very mature way of dealing with models and principles.

Think about physical health: Which recommendations would you see as "principles," which as "models"?

Chapter 3

Understanding "all by itself" growth

Throughout this chapter, we will be dealing with many different principles of church health that have been identified by our research. However, all of these principles have one common denominator: Every single one is targeted at releasing "all by itself" growth. In Natural Church Development, our task is not to make the church grow, but to reduce human-made hindrances to growth. Then the church can flourish "all by itself."

Throughout God's creation we can study how "all by itself" growth works.

My experiences:

The realization that a church already has everything it needs in order to grow has had a dramatic impact on my seminars. To put it into the categories of the "square wheels" cartoon (page 85), I know that it is not my task to push or pull a church. Rather, it is my goal to help it discover the "round wheels" that are already there, and to put them in the right places. Sometimes I look at this cartoon before I enter the room where an NCD conference is going to be held, just to remind myself of what is my job, and what is God's. I know that it will make all the difference in the world whether I see myself in the position of "pushing and pulling," or in the position of helping others discover "round wheels."

"All by itself" growth in the Bible

The term "all by itself" growth goes back to Jesus' teaching on the dynamics of the kingdom of God, as recorded in Mark 4:26-29: "This is what the kingdom of God is like. A man scatters seed on the ground. Night and day, whether he sleeps or gets up, the seed sprouts and grows, though he does not know how. *All by itself* the soil produces grain—first the stalk, then the head, then the full kernel in the head. As soon as the grain is ripe, he puts the sickle to it, because the harvest has come."

This parable clearly shows what people can and should do, and what they cannot do. They should sow and harvest; they may sleep and get up. What they cannot ever do is this: they cannot bring forth the fruit. The text says that the grain grows "all by itself" (in Greek, the term is *automate*). In countless churches, however, we try just the opposite: we strive to make the church grow in our own strength, and in the end we don't have enough energy to do what we *are* supposed to do: the sowing and the harvesting.

Different kinds of growth

There are many churches that are interested in growth, but don't have a well-developed understanding of "all by itself" growth. They are happy with *any* kind of growth, whether it is human or divinely generated, whether it occurs as the fruit of their own energy investment or "all by itself." However, this difference is of utmost spiritual and strategic importance.

It is possible to achieve numerical growth following other means than those taught in this book. We can, in fact, experience growth by constantly increasing the human energy that we invest into the church. The problem with this kind of growth is that it doesn't have any sustainable power. As soon as we reduce our energy investment—because we are frustrated, burned out, or simply need a little rest—there is the danger that the whole ministry will begin to stagnate. In order to experience ongoing growth, this approach demands a constant increase of our energy investment.

This cartoon has become a chief tool for communicating what "all by itself" growth is all about. The "cart with square wheels" symbolizes the situation of Christians who haven't yet discovered this principle. They try, in their own strength, to do what God wants to do for them.

More and more pressure

In my ministry, I have encountered countless varieties of this approach: leadership styles that depend on a 16-hour work day; forms of spirituality that put enormous pressure on church members; ministry expectations that compete with basic family or professional needs; worship services that demand an incredible, almost inhuman level of preparation in order to satisfy the constantly increasing level of expectations.

Don't misunderstand me. I am not saying that all of these activities are worthless and that those involved in them are unspiritual. Usually, they are wonderful people, eager to see results for the kingdom of God. But the problem is that, in their eagerness to see results, maybe even quick results, they have missed the secret of "all by itself" growth.

More on the web:

On the internet (see page 162) you will find answers to the following questions:

• *Are there secular equivalents to "all by itself" growth?*

• *If "all by itself" growth works so well, why do so many Christians follow other approaches?*

"All by itself" growth takes time

Since "all by itself" growth is organic growth, it takes time, just as any organic process takes time. We cannot expect to sow and to harvest in the same day. There are different seasons, in our spiritual lives and in the life of our church just as there are in agriculture, and we must learn to live in accordance with the laws of these seasons.

Does this mean that "slowness" is a good indicator of health? Definitely not. I have encountered many churches that are incredibly slow, not because of their involvement in an organic growth process, but because people procrastinate, evade conflicts, or simply don't do the right things. Slowness in itself is definitely not a virtue. However, whenever people promise us quick results, I would suspect that the dynamics of "all by itself" growth have been overlooked. Many things that bring about quick results have counter-productive effects in the long run.

Doing things differently

It could be that you are reluctant to get involved with NCD because you fear that you will have to invest even more time into church-related activities when you already have more than enough to do. However, the goal of NCD is not to do more things, but to do things differently. Since the decisive difference is nothing other than releasing "all by itself" growth, the end result should be that with less to do than before, you are experiencing greater results.

Organic processes take time in church life, just as they do in nature.

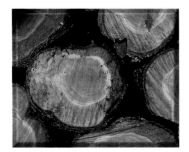

"Wonderful theory," you may think. "But does it really work like this?" On page 12, I mentioned that we had selected all of the churches in our database that had done three or more NCD Surveys to find out what kinds of change actually occurred in the 31 months between survey 1 and survey 3. We learned that, in this time frame, quality grew by 6 points, on average, and the growth rate by 51%, shifting from transfer to conversion growth. For such significant growth in quality and quantity to take place, one might expect that the active church members were paying for it by having more work to do and less down time.

More time for hobbies?

Since we have the data of all of these churches in our computer, we decided to investigate whether or not this was actually true. The questionnaire of the NCD Survey contains 170 items that are used to measure the quality of the church. Some of these items deal with the members' prayer life, others with the use of their spiritual gifts, others with the quality of the worship service, others with small group experiences, etc. For every item, we calculated how strongly the qualitative increase between survey 1 and survey 3 had been.

The item with the second-strongest positive change was the following, "Despite my church activities, I have sufficient time for my hobbies." At the time of the third survey, there were 9.3% more affirmative responses to this statement. There were remarkable changes for most of the other items as well, but none of them were as strong as in this area.

Translating this discovery from the technical categories of the survey into everyday practice, we can conclude that among the positive changes that churches involved with Natural Church Development experience, the most visible is that the active members of the church feel less pressured in their church involvements than they used to. At the same time, they are able to perform their tasks in the church better than before. They are measurably more happy, more fulfilled, and more effective. And they see more fruit. All of this is not achieved by more work, but by less.

Can you see any similarities between the cartoon on page 85 and your church's ministry?

This is an empirically measurable consequence of what "all by itself" growth is about. It is not an abstract theory, but, as all gifts from God, a down-to-earth reality. Thank you, heavenly Father.

Two different sets of principles

O n the next few pages, you will be introduced to all of the principles that make up Natural Church Development. There are two different categories of principles: *six growth forces* (in earlier NCD books they were referred to as "biotic principles"), *and eight quality characteristics* of healthy churches. While the quality characteristics deal with the question, *"What* shall we do?", the six growth forces are focused on the question, *"How* shall we do it?"

In addition to these principles, this book deals with related tools that have been developed to put the NCD principles into practice. I want to stress again that these tools should not be confused with principles. If you regard them as helpful, use them; if not, don't use them. But when it comes to principles it's a different story. You *must* use them. Of course, you could decide against them, but that would not stop them from impacting your life. Principles apply whether you use them or not; they apply even if you purposely reject them. Because of that, it is a wise decision to use them deliberately.

Six growth forces

The table below summarizes the six growth forces. Every single one of them is targeted on releasing "all by itself" growth. In real life, we cannot draw a strict dividing line between the individual principles, as all of them have the same underlying dynamics. The six terms just focus on different aspects of these dynamics.

I have learned all six growth forces by observing God's creation, especially from the vantage points of biology and ecology. For that reason, I have deliberately assigned names to them that remind us of this origin. We should not presume, however, that these are "secular"

The table below summarizes the six growth forces. To learn how to apply these principles, it can be helpful to ask the questions mentioned, whenever you have to make a decision.

Inter-dependence	Multi-plication	Energy transformation
How does this decision affect other areas of life?	*Does this decision contribute to multiplication or merely to addition?*	*Does this decision take advantage of the resources in the environment?*

Six growth forces

Sustain-ability	Symbiosis	Fruitful-ness
Do the results of this decision have built-in mechanisms to sustain themselves?	*Does this decision foster a fruitful co-operation between different activities?*	*Does this decision produce visible fruit for the kingdom of God?*

Empowering leadership	Gift-based ministry	Passionate spirituality	Effective structures
Are your leaders focused on equipping believers for ministry?	*Are tasks in your church distributed according to the criterion of gifting?*	*Is the spiritual life of the church members characterized by passion?*	*Do the structures of your church contribute to growth?*

Eight quality characteristics

Inspiring worship service	Holistic small groups	Need-oriented evangelism	Loving relationships
Are your worship services an inspiring experience for the members?	*Do the small groups address the life issues of their members?*	*Are the evangelistic activities related to the needs of those you are trying to win?*	*Are the relationships of the members characterized by love?*

The above table summarizes the eight quality characteristics of healthy churches. The questions hint at the decisive point behind each of these principles.

concepts that are transferred to the Christian sphere. Who invented these concepts? None other than God, the Creator, the father of Jesus Christ himself. In his wisdom, he has designed all of his creation to function according to these dynamics, including the church. Just as natural laws apply to believers and non-believers alike, so do the six growth forces. A church that has difficulty seeing the spiritual relevance of these principles most likely struggles with the "green zone" of our trinitarian diagram.

Eight quality characteristics

The eight quality characteristics (see table above) have been the direct outcome of our research. These are the qualities that all growing churches have in common, regardless of cultural, theological, and size differences. Growing churches rank considerably higher in each of the eight areas than stagnating and declining ones.

Which of these principles have you already seen in action?

As we will see later, it is not possible to separate the six growth forces from the eight quality characteristics. In fact, it is the very essence of each of the quality characteristics that the growth forces are put into practice. In other words, we have to approach all of these principles as being interrelated. It's not possible to choose our "favorite" principle and to disregard the others. It is a characteristic feature of NCD not to promote one specific point, but to strive for harmony among all of the principles of church development. This is because "balance" is such an important ingredient of health.

Six growth forces

The broad acceptance of NCD's eight quality characteristics can be attributed, in part, to a misunderstanding. The eight nouns (leadership, ministry, spirituality, etc.) sound so generic that everyone can identify with them. What many people overlook, however, is the specific twist that the corresponding adjectives (empowering, gift-based, passionate, etc.) communicate. While we can find the nouns in almost every church, it is only in healthy churches that we can find the adjectives.

If you take a closer look at the adjectives, you will realize that each of them strives to express what we have called the six growth forces. For instance, what do we mean by empowering leadership? It's shorthand for an approach to leadership that strives to release the growth forces of interdependence, multiplication, energy transformation, sustainability, symbiosis, and fruitfulness. The same idea applies to the other seven quality characteristics as well.

The "N" of NCD

Recently a bishop of a large denomination told me, "I like your eight quality characteristics very much. We practice them in most of our churches. What we don't like so much, is your teaching on the six growth forces." I asked him, "How can you like the quality characteristics if you don't like the growth forces? Releasing the growth forces is what the quality characteristics are all about." He said, "We have our own ideas for addressing the eight areas that are far better accepted than your 'all by itself' philosophy."

When the bishop shared about the methods that they had used, it became clear that they had basically continued doing what they had been doing for decades (without seeing a lot of fruit), but that now they had organized the same activities and even the same mistakes around the names of the eight quality characteristics. I have discovered this to be a frequent trap: People use the aspects of NCD that they feel comfortable with, and the end result is nothing other than a reorganization of their old, bad habits around new terminology. If we take the six growth forces out of NCD, we reduce Natural Church Development to Church Development—we erase the "N" from NCD.

Learning from the "lilies of the field"

When Jesus spoke about the dynamics of the kingdom of God, he seldom missed the opportunity to stress the importance of the "N." He constantly referred to nature—the lilies of the field, the seed that grows by itself, the growth of the

When Jesus spoke about the dynamics of God's kingdom, he continually referred to nature.

My experiences:

When teaching about the six growth forces, I sometimes hear pastors of growing churches say that they don't apply these principles, they just preach the Word of God. Whenever I hear this, I usually invite them to come forward for an interview. During these interviews it becomes crystal clear to the audience that these pastors actually do apply these principles, without realizing it. On one humorous occasion, we had the funny situation of a pastor who accused me of "heresy" because of my teaching on the six growth forces, until our interview revealed that he himself had applied these principles all of his life.

mustard seed, the four soils, the tree and its fruit, the laws of sowing and reaping. A typical example of his teaching can be found in Matthew 6:28: "See how the lilies of the field grow." The word "see," however, does not fully cover the implications of the Greek word *katamathete*, which is the intensive form of *manthano*, meaning to learn, observe, study, or research. In Greek, whenever *kata* is used in front of a verb, it usually intensifies its meaning. So *katamathete* means to *diligently* learn, observe, study, or research.

What, then, are we to diligently study? Not the lilies' beauty, but rather their growth mechanisms. We are to study them, examine them, meditate on them, and take our direction from them—all these aspects are included in the imperative verb form *katamathete*. We are told that we need to do these things in order to understand the principles of the kingdom of God.

> **Pastors of growing churches face the same challenges as others, but they see endless growth potential where others only see problems.**

How we studied the growth forces

This is what we have done in Natural Church Development. We encountered the six growth forces everywhere in God's creation, most easily accessible through biology and ecology. We saw them at work in thousands of churches around the globe when we did our research. And Scripture supplied us with never-ending illustrations of how God has built his kingdom, including the church, through these forces.

I have discovered that while Eastern and Southern cultures tend to be more receptive to this approach, Western cultures have difficulty understanding the growth forces. This is a reflection of the limitations of linear thinking that is predominant in the Western world. It is excellent for understanding technical realities, but not sufficient when it comes to "all by itself" growth. In this area, the Western world can learn both from the East, with its bi-polar thought structure, and the South with its circular, cyclical orientation (see page 28).

How to develop a "sixth sense"

On the next few pages, I will further explain the six growth forces. For each principle I will suggest three practical steps. If you have difficulty understanding some of the principles, don't worry. Understanding every single one is not as important as developing a growing *sense* for the underlying dynamic of all six growth forces.

More on the web:

On the internet (see page 162) you will find answers to the following questions:

• *Are there training programs that focus on learning how to apply these principles?*

• *Why are these principles so seldom taught at seminaries and universities?*

Pastors of growing churches have usually developed this sense. Sometimes it almost appears as a "sixth sense." They face the same challenges as others, yet they see endless growth potential where others only see problems. In many cases, they may not even be aware of it, but

Fruitfulness

Interdependence

"All by itself" growth

Multiplication

Symbiosis

Sustainability

Energy transformation

The six growth forces are most powerful when they work in harmony with one another. Every single force contributes to "all by itself" growth.

what they are constantly doing is releasing God's growth forces. It is so normal, so natural for them, that they don't even have to think about it. The growth forces have become their second nature.

Moving to a new paradigm

If you are one of those people who apply these principles without really thinking about it, you will probably enjoy the next few pages because they describe what you have been doing without ever having considered it from this perspective.

However, you may be a reader who comes from the opposite starting point. You may realize that you don't naturally act in accordance with the six growth forces. The good news is that everyone can learn this art. I have seen purely linear, technocratic thinkers gradually become "all by itself" thinkers. It takes time, of course, but it is very rewarding. It will not only help you in your church activities, but literally in all areas of your life. Rather than increasing your own energy level, you will learn to utilize the energies that God has already provided. If the "lilies of the field" can do it, you can do it, too.

To what degree, would you say, do you already live in accordance with the six growth forces?

Growth force 1: Interdependence

O ne of the great miracles of God's creation is the interdependence of its parts, from the minutest microorganisms to the most magnificent stars. Viewing a phenomenon in the context of its manifold relationships rather than in isolation is what the Scriptures call "wisdom."

All the elements of God's creation are connected with each other.

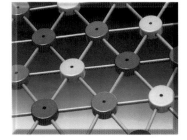

My experiences:

Studying the principle of interdependence gave me the initial ideas for how to develop our own organization: as a network of hundreds of interrelated units. People who are accustomed to thinking exclusively in hierarchies sometimes have difficulty understanding our organizational structure and label our ministry as "independent." But there is hardly a description that is more misleading than that. The basic structure of the NCD Community is not independent, but interdependent. Since interdependence releases "all by itself" growth, it's no surprise to me that the international ministry has grown so quickly. An interdependent structure is far more powerful than a hierarchical (dependent) or an independent ministry could ever be.

No church can afford to ignore the growth force of interdependence. We can study its effects when we analyze churches that have done repeat NCD Surveys. Whenever a church works on one of the eight quality characteristics, not only does the point value change in that area, but it also tends to change in all of the others as well. Working on the quality characteristic of gift-based ministry, for example, significantly influences other areas, including leadership, spirituality, structures, and relationships.

Step 1: Be skeptical about short-term success

Probably the greatest enemy of this force is our preoccupation with short-term success, which reduces our perspective to one element, without seeing its interrelatedness with all other elements. If you follow this path, you may actually see quick results in one area, but chances are good that, since the other areas have been overlooked, the long-term outcome will be counterproductive.

To help you understand these dynamics, compare the offer of a "miracle pill" with the development of a healthy life-style, including a balanced diet, physical exercise, and spiritual training. Which one will have the more lasting effect? Definitely the healthy life-style. Which one will be more popular? The pill. And if this specific pill doesn't work, we will try another one tomorrow. After all, we want quick results.

Step 2: Create an awareness of side effects

Linear thinking would make us believe that every action we take has only one effect, the desired one. This is far from true. When you do something, there are literally hundreds of effects, visible and invisible, positive and negative, intended and surprising. Most of us have yet to learn how to anticipate these side effects. In many countries, when the pharmaceutical industry sells medicine, they are required to explain the possible side effects as well as the desired effects. It would be beneficial to develop something similar for spiritual medicine as well.

There is no church development recipe that is good "in and of itself." Is it good to hire a full-time evangelist? Sometimes yes, sometimes no. The wonderful ministry of the new full-

In God's creation, microcosm and macrocosm cannot be separated from each other. Since everything is inter-connected, changes in one area will impact many other areas.

time evangelist could have the negative side-effect that church members delegate their own evangelistic responsibility to him. Is a "seeker service" good or bad? The same answer applies. It can be a wonderful way of con-necting a worship experience with a specific form of evangelism; but it can also be counterproductive if that approach does not fit the church's culture or gift-mix. The same can be said about prayer styles, fund-raising techniques, Bible-study tools, and whole church models. Without evaluat-ing the side-effects, it's impossible to evaluate the desired main effect.

Step 3: Keep the "whole package" of NCD in mind

Some time ago, a pastor complained that NCD doesn't work. "We have already read two of your books," he told me, "and our church still doesn't grow." Obviously he had confused reading a book with implementing the principles. There is a serious danger of confusing the individual ele-ments of NCD with "miracle pills," rather than seeing NCD as a system of many interrelated elements (see page 17). Of course, you can enter the system by picking up any one of its elements. NCD is deliberately designed that way. However, when you are dealing with one specific ele-ment, make sure that you never lose the big picture. That is why *Color Your World with Natural Church Development* introduces you to the whole system, and not just to some selected popular features.

In what ways have you seen the principle of inter-dependence at work in your life?

Growth force 2: Multiplication

Chapter 3

I n God's creation, unlimited growth is unnatural. A tree doesn't grow bigger and bigger; it brings forth new trees, which in turn produce more trees. This is the principle of multiplication that God has implanted into all of his creation.

In God's creation, all living things have been designed to multiply.

My experiences:

At 6'4", I am quite tall and a little bit too heavy (211 pounds). Whenever I sense that people don't understand the difference between addition and multiplication growth, I use my own body as an illustration. I tell them, "In my youth, I grew quickly, and by my 17th birthday I had reached my full height. After that, I regretfully grew a little bit too much in the other dimension, but due to regular exercise I was able to keep it within limits. However, I am extremely thankful to God that my growth stopped at a given point. Rather than building an endlessly growing fat-and-ugly 'mega Schwarz,' God had a better plan for me. There are three wonderful-looking 'mini Schwarzes' in our house. That's multiplication in contrast with addition." Looking at my heavy body, people usually get the point immediately.

While the term multiplication doesn't appear in Scripture, the Bible gives us countless illustrations of how God has used this principle. The best example is Jesus' ministry. He invested himself primarily in his disciples, who in turn were commissioned to make disciples who were to make more disciples. What is the Great Commission if not a call for ongoing multiplication!

Step 1: Realize that the opposite of multiplication is addition

In mathematics, the opposite of multiplication is division. In church development, however, a different logic applies. The real opposite of a "multiplication mindset" is an "addition mindset." Addition means striving to enlarge an existing organization by adding more elements to it: $2 + 2 + 2 + 2 + 2$. Multiplication, on the other hand, means striving to give birth to new organisms, that themselves will contribute to the birth of new organisms: $2 \times 2 \times 2 \times 2 \times 2$.

A growth process based on addition quickly reaches natural limits. A growth process based on multiplication, however, is exclusively limited by the counterforces of the environment.

Step 2: Accept "death" as a normal aspect of life

Years ago, when dealing with a complicated situation in a large denomination, I suggested that a number of churches should be closed. The emotions that were triggered by that suggestion were explosive. "And we thought your field of expertise was church growth, not church death," one of the denominational leaders shouted at me. "You want to kill our churches," another one added. Nobody actually shouted "Murderer!", but I am sure that the majority were thinking just that.

In many denominations around the globe it's still taboo to think about closing a church, a ministry, or a group. When thinking about God's creation, however, this should be one of the most natural things in the world. Where multiplication processes are functioning, straightforward talk about "death" is also permitted. Why should groups or churches not be allowed to die after they have run their course? This thought should not be threatening at all if the church or group has given life to four children, 16 grandchildren and 54 great-grandchildren. In God's creation, individual organisms die, but the genetic information remains and reproduces itself.

Imagine a water lily growing in a pond. At the beginning of the year the water lily has exactly one leaf. After one week there are two leaves. A week later, four. After sixteen weeks half of the water's surface is covered with leaves. How long will it take before the second half is covered? Another sixteen weeks? No, just one more week. That is how multiplication works.

Do you know what the long-term goal of NCD International is? On a given day, we will invite our partners and "bury" our organization in a celebrative act. That day will be one of our final contributions to "all by itself" growth and, if well prepared, that growth will be sustainable.

Step 3: Remember that the true fruit of an apple tree is not an apple, but another apple tree

It was Donald McGavran, the father of the church growth movement, who taught me this principle. "What is the true fruit of an apple tree?", he asked me, curiously waiting for my response. At that time I was naïve enough to answer, "It's an apple, of course." It seemed as if McGavran was just waiting for that answer. "Wrong," he said, as he paused meaningfully. "The true fruit of an apple tree is not an apple, but another apple tree." McGavran wanted to make it crystal-clear that this concept was meant to be life-changing for me.

It took me a number of years before I realized the wisdom of this simple statement. If the true fruit of an apple tree is not an apple, but another apple tree, then the true fruit of a small group is not a new Christian, but another group; and the true fruit of an evangelist is not a convert, but new evangelists; and the true fruit of a church is not a new group, but another church; and the true fruit of a leader is not followers, but new leaders. Indeed, that *is* a life-changing message. Thank you, Donald McGavran, for helping me discover this divine principle!

In what ways have you seen the principle of multiplication at work in your life?

Growth force 3: Energy transformation

Health-destroying energies are transformed into health-promoting ones.

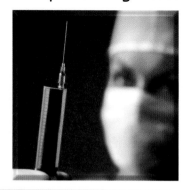

My experiences:

Since I have to travel a lot, a vast part of my time is absorbed in waiting. For years I complained about that. Everything changed the moment I started to apply the principle of energy transformation. I have developed countless techniques for using this time creatively. Frequently, I use it to study foreign languages, since I can repeat memorized structures even when standing in a line. In that way, I have been able to develop an elementary understanding of more than 20 languages. When coming home from a trip, my wife used to say, "I hope you haven't had too many waiting times." Now she says, "I hope you have had a lot of time to wait." She knows how valuable these creative times have become for me.

I f I were allowed to select only one NCD principle and declare it my "favorite principle" (though I told you that we should never do that), I definitely would choose this one: the growth force of energy transformation. The power behind this principle is so dramatic that I can only assign it to the fact that God himself has designed it in his wisdom.

We frequently encounter this principle in Scripture. One of the most famous examples is the way Paul, on the Areopagus, referred to the "unknown god" (obviously an idol) and made it the point of departure for his evangelistic sermon in Athens (Acts 17). God's use of the persecution of Christians (Acts 8) to advance the Gospel is another variation on this principle. The blood of martyrs becomes the seed of the church. Hostile energy is thus transformed into holy energy.

The same principle can be studied by observing nature. It's exactly the way an organism fights a virus. Viruses generally make us sick, therefore they are bad. However, in small doses they cause the body to counteract and strengthen its immune system. That is how vaccinations work. Health-destroying energies are transformed through the vaccination process into health-promoting ones.

Step 1: Identify supporting and opposing forces

Since the whole point of this principle is to use the energy of your environment, you first have to identify what the energy situation is. What are the supporting and opposing forces in terms of your specific goal? When asking this question, you will probably come up with a lot of issues which could arguably be either "supporting" or "opposing" forces: trends in society, political decisions, economic developments, existing conflicts, etc. According to the logic of energy transformation, many of the apparently opposing forces may actually support the Christian cause.

Step 2: Stop fighting against opposing forces

Of course you can choose to fight against opposing forces, and many of these fights may be more than justified. This will, however, cost you a lot of energy, and at the end of the battle you will have to ask yourself how much you have actually achieved. Many of the opposing forces in our environment cannot be changed anyway. As each of us only has limited resources, we should utilize them as wisely as possible. If we have already invested them in battles that cannot be won, there is the danger that we won't have enough energy left to address the third and most important step.

This is a picture of the windmills behind our house in Emmelsbüll, Germany. Actually, these windmills don't produce energy; they just transform the energy that is plentifully available in our area: wind. In our part of Germany, we usually experience the wind as "hostile energy." The windmills transform it into useful energy: electricity.

Step 3: Utilize the opponent's energy for the kingdom

At our first NCD Global Summit in South Africa, Eddie Leo, a representative for the Indonesian NCD Partner, shared about the revival that our Indonesian friends are experiencing. Among other things, he reported that within the preceding six months, God had added 1,600 believers to their local church. Many of the other NCD National Partners were interested in his story. They wanted to know what they could do in order to experience a similar revival. "You want revival?", Eddie asked them. "Then pray for persecution." When saying this, Eddie gave us his most friendly Indonesian smile, but he meant it as the bitter truth.

Without a doubt, the persecution that our Indonesian friends are undergoing—and I am not speaking just about breaking church window panes, but *real* persecution—is one of the driving forces behind the revival. They have learned to creatively use this hostile energy for the kingdom.

We should be careful, however, not to relate the principle of energy transformation exclusively to dramatic situations. It's a down-to-earth principle that applies to literally all areas of our lives—to how we deal with time waiting in airports, conflicts within our churches, financial difficulties, as well as with lack of motivation. The constant question is this: How can we best use this situation to advance God's kingdom? This is a very creative question, and it is a very biblical one. The promise in Romans 8:28 reads, "We know that in all things God works for the good of those who love him."

In what ways have you seen the principle of energy transformation at work in your life?

Chapter 3

Growth force 4: Sustainability

By God's design, the natural fruit of every living organism contains the seed for its reproduction. Since natural reproduction follows the principle of multiplication, not addition (see page 94), sustainability contributes to dramatic growth.

When you live in step with this force, you no longer have to think about growth.

My experiences:

Before we got married, my wife Brigitte worked in an orphanage in India. When she arrived, the childrens' diet was exclusively rice and pepper water. Once a week, Brigitte bought an egg for each child, which quickly became the highlight of the week. Once a month, they were even able to afford a chicken for the whole group. Three months before Brigitte had to leave India, she began to wonder how these things would continue. So instead of buying another chicken and more eggs, she bought two living hens and a cock. Half a year after she had left India, the kids had eggs three times a week, and chicken once a week. Training the kids to breed chickens has had more sustainable power than all of the eggs and chickens previously purchased.

Given the fact that your resources are limited, you should apply this principle wisely. Once it is implemented, you will no longer have to divide your energy between these two areas:

1. The actual results you want to achieve by means of a certain activity (the *fruit*).

2. The maintenance and growth of your ministry (the *seed*).

In God's creation, the same energy simultaneously produces the results *and* the maintenance, the fruit *and* the seed. In fact, according to God's design, the results equal the maintenance, and the fruit is equivalent to the seed. If you live in step with this force, you won't have to think about the maintenance and growth of your church (area 2) any longer. Why not? Because it happens all by itself. It's the natural outcome of what you have done in area 1.

Step 1: Check every fruit for seeds

The less you follow the natural dynamics described in this book, the greater the likelihood that the "fruit" that you produce won't have any bearing on the maintenance of your ministry. You might produce wonderful flowers, but when they begin to wilt you will be unable to find seeds in them.

Consider this concept as it relates to the area of finances. Often people invest money into (1) the results they want to achieve by means of a certain activity, and (2) the upkeep of their ministry, which is the base for future activities. However, if the ministry were designed in harmony with the growth force of sustainability, they would only have to invest in number 1 and not even think about number 2. This principle explains why we, at NCD International, consistently reject donations. Rather, the natural fruit of our ministry must take care of its financial needs. For that reason, there are no fundraising or PR departments in NCD International. One-hundred percent of the existing energy is invested into the actual results we want to achieve.

Step 2: Use every opportunity to train others

It is extremely revealing to observe how Jesus applied this principle. He didn't have separate programs for discipleship training and public ministry. Rather, he trained his disciples by ministering to people. This kind of on-the-job training guaranteed

Flowers are beautiful, but that is not their most important function in God's creation. Every flower contains the capacity to sustain its species. When the flower is at the peak of its beauty, this capacity is hardly visible. As soon as it starts to wilt, however, the seeds can be seen.

a high quality of training with hardly any additional energy investment. Jesus knew how to make the wisest use of his limited time on earth.

The same principle can be observed in healthy churches. They don't have leaders, on the one hand, who invest their energies in leadership alone, and training programs, on the other hand, to develop new leaders. Instead, new leaders are trained as they actually participate in leadership. Once you have learned how to use every opportunity to train other people, you start to release the power of sustainability.

Step 3: Don't solve people's problems; help them to solve them on their own

You probably know the famous saying, "Give a man a fish and you feed him for a day; teach a man to fish and you feed him for a lifetime." That is what sustainability is all about. Far too many things in the Christian world are focused on offering people fish (solutions to their problems), rather than teaching them how to fish (finding the solutions themselves). In NCD, we strive to apply this principle consistently. This explains why NCD tools don't offer step-by-step instructions applicable for all situations. Rather, we offer universal principles and invest our energy teaching people how to apply them. In that way, people are enabled to find appropriate solutions on their own.

In what ways have you seen the principle of sustainability at work in your life?

Growth force 5: Symbiosis

Symbiosis, according to Webster's Dictionary, is "the intimate living together of two dissimilar organisms in a mutually beneficial relationship." In this definition, both elements are important: (1) the "dissimilarity" of the two organisms and (2) their "mutually beneficial relationship." If one of these two elements is neglected, the principle of symbiosis cannot release its power.

> **The enemies of symbiosis are monoculture and competition.**

Current management literature refers to this principle as "win-win relationships." Rather than having winners and losers, decisions are made in such a way that everyone wins. Though some management theorists celebrate this insight as a novelty (and maybe in some branches of management this really has been a new insight), a win-win relationship is in essence not different from the "Golden Rule" which Jesus taught 2000 years ago. However, he did not call it "win-win" or "symbiosis," but, "Love your neighbor as yourself."

Step 1: Avoid both monoculture and competition

Two negative models stand in contrast to this principle: competition and monoculture. Competition assumes "dissimilar organisms," just like symbiosis does, but these organisms harm rather than help one another. Monoculture, on the other hand (called monopolism in economy, society, and church life), has lost the variety of species, and one type of organism dominates. This obviously eliminates destructive competition, but it also takes away the mutually beneficial relationship between different species.

You can relate this principle to all areas of church life. Take, for instance, such differing themes as "ecumenism," "small groups," "spiritual gifts," "devotional styles," and "inter-cultural encounters." In all of these areas, you can easily identify believers who tend to have a monopolistic perspective and strive for uniformity. Others stress values like independence and variety and end up in competition. According to Webster's definition of symbiosis, one group stresses the first pillar; the other, the second pillar. But both of them are unable to see that the combination of the two dimensions is the key.

Step 2: Appreciate diversity

When I talked about this principle at a conference in Japan, one of the pastors told me, "You were absolutely right in what you were saying. Regretfully, people are so different. As leaders, we have to accept this." My response was, "Thank you for expressing your agreement with me, but please accept my apology for not agreeing with you. It is not *regretful* that people are different; it is God's plan. And we don't just have to

My experiences:

Our NCD network functions well because the people involved in it are extremely different in mentality, culture, and theological convictions. This is even true for the two leaders of the network, my colleague Christoph Schalk and myself. We are extremely different in almost every single aspect of our lives. However, since both of us know what symbiosis is all about, neither of us complains that the other person feels, thinks, and acts so differently from how he would feel, think, and act. We simply know that we need to be different in order to minister effectively to so many different needs. And we know that by applying the principle of symbiosis in our leadership team, we are contributing to "all by itself" growth in the whole network.

Symbiosis depends on a variety of different organisms living in the same place. Of course, a monocultural approach is able to produce impressive amounts of fruit as well. However, since monoculture is blind to the stabilizing effects of hedges, swamps, and horticultural variety, the overall energy investment in terms of artificial fertilizers, pesticides, etc. is far higher.

accept this, but to appreciate it, to rejoice in it, to celebrate it." As long as we just "accept" the inevitable fact of diversity, while in our hearts we dream of a church with monopolistic, uniform patterns, we are still far away from understanding the true meaning of symbiosis.

Step 3: Network different approaches so that they benefit from each other

Diversity in itself—the first pillar in Webster's definition—doesn't lead us anywhere. The challenge is to network different approaches in a way that every participant experiences the benefits. Look again at the different themes mentioned above: ecumenism, small groups, spiritual gifts, devotional styles, inter-cultural encounters. In every single case, diversity can lead to fights and, in the case of inter-cultural encounters, even to wars, if the different approaches are not related to each other.

It is, in fact, a difficult task to do this, in politics as well as in church life. However, this is what leadership is all about. A true leader doesn't take sides with one of the competing groups, but strives to help each group realize how a symbiotic relationship will be more beneficial for each of the different parties. In our NCD network, applying this principle has become a matter of life and death. Since the cultures, styles, and theological convictions of the groups involved are so extremely different, a major part of our ministry is to show what it means in practical terms to apply the principle of symbiosis.

In what ways have you seen the principle of symbiosis at work in your life?

Growth force 6: Fruitfulness

Measuring long-term fruit is a fitting way to assess the health of an organism.

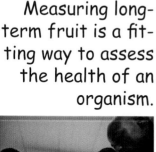

My experiences:

Once a year, I meet with my colleague Christoph Schalk to evaluate the twelve preceding months of ministry. As far as I can remember, we haven't once asked to what degree our organization has expanded. Neither of us shows the slightest interest in pursuing this question. But what we do ask is to what extent the ministry has increased. Every year we want to see measurably more fruit than in the preceding year. If that should not occur, we immediately and dramatically change our own work (usually by cutting things out), as we firmly believe it is our responsibility as leaders to contribute to ever-increasing fruitfulness.

All living things in God's creation are characterized by their ability to bear fruit. There are, of course, situations in which no fruit—or not enough fruit—is produced. But in every single case this is an indication that things are not working as they should. Measuring long-term fruit is a fitting way to assess the health of a given organism.

It is not a coincidence that Jesus repeatedly referred to this natural law and applied it to the spiritual realm. In Matthew 7 we read, "Every good tree bears good fruit" and, "By their fruit you will recognize them" (verses 17 and 16). Whenever Scripture speaks about fruit, it is referring to visible manifestations, even if they might have invisible roots. Since fruit is visible, it is possible to examine it. The principle of fruitfulness is concerned with this evaluation. Following three simple steps will help make your life more fruitful.

Step 1: Name the fruit

Start by asking the question, *What do we want to achieve?* In order to measure the fruit later on (step 3), you need to know from the outset what kind of fruit you are after. If you had wanted to harvest potatoes, you shouldn't be presenting apples from an apple tree as if they were the desired fruit. Believe it or not, doing just that is a favorite game for many Christians when they speak about spiritual fruit.

For instance, if a church is planning an evangelistic campaign, they need to define beforehand what kind of fruit they would like to see in terms of people won for Christ. If, as a result of the campaign, the fellowship of the believers has been strengthened but no one has been won for Christ, they can still rejoice in the better quality of their fellowship, but they should not confuse it with the fruit of the campaign. Very likely, they could have achieved that result far better through some other means.

Step 2: Plan for fruit

Once you have defined what you would like to achieve, ask the following question: *How do we want to achieve it?* This sequence is of crucial importance. Only ask the second question after you have clearly defined your goal. It is important, of course, to plan in harmony with the growth forces described in this book. If you plan for fruit (rather than for a machine), you have to apply the principles of life, rather than the laws of technology.

Let's assume you are planning an evangelistic campaign. It is possible to follow either technocratic procedures or to focus on releasing the growth forces. In the first case, you might

In God's creation, bearing fruit is a sign of life. If a vine does not bear fruit, it has to be cut down. Not surprisingly, Scripture gives us the same instructions when it comes to spiritual fruit (John 15:1-8).

start by collecting the necessary funds for carrying out the campaign. You might exclusively focus on "big names" to guarantee success. You might be tempted to use manipulative techniques to get enough converts. However, if you follow the organic principles of life, you might develop creative ways to reach your goal without any money. You will be attentive to natural multiplication processes. You will not be merely interested in "decisions for Christ," but in life-long changes. You will plan for sustainable fruit.

Step 3: Test the fruit

Never forget to ask the third question, *To what extent have we reached our goal?* If you discover that you are not as fruitful as you should or could be, follow the biblical instruction to "prune" (John 15:1-4) in order to increase your fruitfulness.

These three steps apply to all areas of life, as we are challenged to bear fruit in all areas of our lives, not just in the context of our church involvements. Making the three questions part of your life-style will help you become a more fruitful person.

The principle of fruitfulness plays a central role in Natural Church Development. The NCD Survey, for instance, has been designed as an instrument to measure the quality of the church (step 3). The results will help you set specific goals for desired qualitative increase in the decisive areas (step 1) and develop plans for how to reach these goals in harmony with the six growth forces (step 2). Later on, you can do another survey to evaluate the degree to which you have reached your goals (step 3). As in nature, applying the principle of fruitfulness is not really a three-step process, but a never-ending cycle.

In what ways have you seen the principle of fruitfulness at work in your life?

Chapter 3

Eight quality characteristics

When reading a book on a subject that relates to one of the eight quality characteristics you will make a confusing discovery. The majority of authors tend to sell you their insights into a specific area as *the* key to church growth. When you read a book on leadership, you will learn that leadership is *the* key. When you read a book on evangelism, the message will be that evangelism is *the* key. And when you pick up a book on small groups, you know even before you open the front cover what will be presented as *the* key...

Eight different keys

There are only two ways to interpret this phenomenon. Either the majority of these authors are wrong, since what one presents as "the" key usually contradicts the key that the other presents. Or all of these authors are right, because each of them does present an essential key to church growth, their mistake simply being that, rather than relating the different keys to each other, they exclusively focus on one key (which is fine) and present it as the only one (which is not so fine).

The simple truth is that there is not *one* key to church growth, but at least eight different keys. If an author should try to make you believe that there is just one key, I would like to encourage you to do the following:

1. Don't be taken in by this message, as it clearly contradicts both biblical and empirical truth.

2. Learn as much as you can from the insights that the author has gained in his or her field of expertise, as this will enable you to discover many valuable insights.

"All you need is prayer"

The tendency to reduce the eight keys to one single factor is as widespread as Christianity itself. When I did an NCD conference in Korea, one of the pastors told me, "The only thing that we do for church growth is pray." When we later looked at the NCD Survey of his church, we discovered that there had indeed been a lot of prayer, as indicated by a high value in "passionate spirituality," but the high values in most of the other seven areas clearly revealed that the church was doing a lot of other things as well. For instance, they were evangelizing (quality characteristic 7), they were practicing spiritual gifts (quality characteristic 2), they were gathering in small groups (quality characteristic 6), they were loving one another (quality characteristic 8).

Thank God, they were doing all of these things, because the Bible clearly teaches us to do them. Nowhere in the Bible do we find the strange message that the only thing we can do for

---

There isn't one key to church growth, but at least eight different keys.

My experiences:

Sometimes people complain that certain dimensions of Christian ministry are not included in the eight quality characteristics. My response is, "If I were a pastor of a local church, I would certainly do many things that are not included on our list, simply because I believe the Bible commands us to." The reason why we did not add those points to our list is that we very neutrally defined as "quality characteristics of growing churches" only those features that showed a universal, positive correlation to numerical growth. If I had defined such a list according to my own theological taste, I certainly would have added a number of other factors. The strength of our list, however, is that it exclusively features objectively verifiable growth principles.

Releasing the six growth forces	Ministry area
Empowering	leadership
Gift-based	ministry
Passionate	spirituality
Effective	structures
Inspiring	worship service
Holistic	small groups
Need-oriented	evangelism
Loving	relationships

Each quality characteristic consists of an adjective (column A) and a noun (column B). As we have seen before (page 89), the adjectives are focused on releasing the six growth forces. They are the key to understanding each of the eight quality characteristics.

church growth is to pray. Unlike many popular books, Scripture doesn't reduce everything to one key. The Bible offers many different keys, and prayer is definitely one of them. It is absolutely essential for church growth, as this Korean pastor rightly stressed. However, the same holds true for each of the other seven quality characteristics as well.

Biblical principles

Since the Bible clearly teaches about each of the eight quality characteristics, why are we so reluctant in NCD to label them as "biblical principles?" Basically, for two reasons. First, while studying this subject I have encountered so many lists of "biblical principles" that better reflected the theological convictions of a given author than universal principles from the Bible, that I wanted to avoid presenting the eight quality characteristics as another attempt along this line.

Second, we did *not* identify these principles through Bible study. We have studied thousands of churches around the globe, as neutrally as possible, and have asked what features growing churches have in common. We did not do this in an attempt to prove our own favorite ideas that had been shaped by our own understanding of the Bible. We did it with an open mindset to learn what is empirically verifiable. The result, however, was that the "secrets of success" revealed by the most comprehensive research that has ever been done on this subject, is nothing other than what the Bible communicated to us long ago. Interesting, isn't it?

More on the web:

On the internet (see page 162) you will find answers to the following questions:

• *Isn't it possible that there is also a ninth or tenth quality characteristic?*

• *Do you have a report that describes the empirical methods applied in this research?*

Which of the eight quality characteristics is your favorite one? Why?

Chapter 3

Quality characteristic 1: Empowering leadership

Please notice that the first quality characteristic is not called "empowered" but "empowering" leadership. Let me explain the difference. "Empowered leadership" could imply that there is one ingenious, multi-talented leader with great vision, who needs volunteers to help him turn his vision into reality.

The superstar model

Outside the Christian realm this concept is sometimes known as "guru leadership." Similar models can be found in Christian churches as well. Some people even uphold this concept as an especially effective growth principle—the guru leader with the great vision on one hand and, the lay troops, who willingly serve their powerful leader as he fulfills his life dreams, on the other.

Our research reveals that this could not be further from the truth. Leaders of growing churches consider it one of their most important tasks to empower others. They equip, support, motivate, and mentor individuals to become all that God wants them to be. Some of these individuals may even be led in a different direction than their leaders. Empowering leaders can rejoice about such a situation with all their heart because they know that God has a unique calling for every individual.

It's interesting to notice that many of the pastors whose churches have had the highest scores on our survey are hardly known among the wider public. Yet they are the ones who provide more helpful basic principles of leadership than many of the world-famous spiritual "superstars." Leaders of growing churches don't have to be superstars. If someone plays this role (or has to play this role because the church expects it), it is usually a sure sign that something is not right in that church.

Explanation, motivation, liberation

Take a look at the diagram on page 107. It shows three essential ingredients of empowering leadership: explanation, motivation, and liberation. If just one of these dimensions is missing, the whole church will suffer. The ability to *explain* complicated realities to people—in sermons, Bible studies, or teaching sessions, for instance—is a great gift from God. However, many people who have this gift have never learned how to *motivate* people. They seriously believe that explaining a certain task is all that people need. And many of those who are able to combine explanation and motivation, are not daring enough to *liberate* their people. Rather, they view them as helpers to fulfill their own (the leader's) vision. They maintain a level of control that makes it impossible for other people to release

> When you encounter an empowering leader, you sense that you are growing.

My experiences:

A church of 900 people in Canada identified empowering leadership as their minimum factor. Since the pastor had been influenced by a widespread teaching on "strong leadership," he understood that he was part of the problem and was even willing to resign. "I am definitely not that kind of a strong leader," he told me. However, an NCD coach convinced him that empowering leadership is not the same as "strong leadership," and that he definitely had the skills necessary for being an empowering leader. For 18 months, the leadership team focused on this issue and experienced considerable quality increase. In the same 18 months, the congregation grew in number to 1700 people.

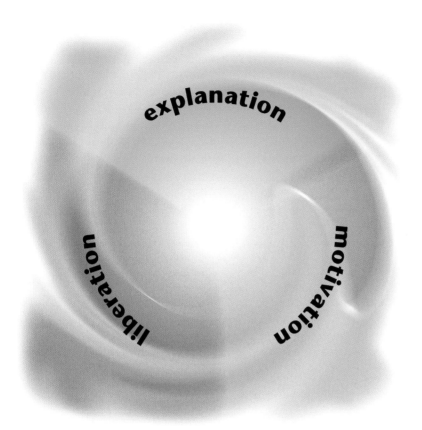

The secret of empowering leadership is (a) to increase the quality in the areas of explanation, motivation, and liberation, and (b) to bring these three dimensions into balance.

their full potential. Liberation means investing yourself into people so that they can fulfill their God-given visions.

Your personal contribution

If you are a leader, focus your ministry on empowering others. Resist the role of the superstar. Find out which of the three areas (explanation, motivation, liberation) is your weakest one and strive for growth in that area. It is important to keep in mind that none of the eight quality characteristics is as easy to improve as empowering leadership—provided that the leadership team is willing to do it.

If you are not a leader, it is your responsibility to look for leaders who will empower you. A first step could be to select a personal mentor who helps you release the potential that God has implanted in you. There is an easy way to discover whether or not someone is an empowering leader. When you are in the presence of an empowering leader, you sense that you are growing. Encountering a "superstar" leader has the opposite effect: While the leader might grow in your eyes, you will feel increasingly smaller.

What has been the most inspiring case study of empowering leadership that you have encountered?

Chapter 3

Quality characteristic 2: Gift-based ministry

The second quality characteristic is based on the conviction that God has already determined who should assume each ministry within the church. The role of the leadership is to help its members identify their gifts and find or create ministries that match them. When you live in harmony with your spiritual gifting, you are no longer ministering in your own strength, but the Holy Spirit is working in you. Thus, even though you may be an ordinary person you can accomplish extraordinary things.

Gift-based ministry enables ordinary people to accomplish extraordinary things.

The cart with the square wheels

Our research revealed the sad fact that most Christians are either not involved in any ministry or function in a ministry that does not match their gifts. Do you remember the cart with the square wheels (page 85)? A person who assumes a task that is outside his or her giftedness resembles one of these square wheels. And a Christian who doesn't have any task in the church? Such a person resembles one of those many unused round wheels in the cart. You can probably imagine what a Christian is like who actually functions in a ministry that matches his or her giftedness. No wonder the practical application of this principle has such dramatic results for the growth of the church!

One of the interesting corollary results of our research was the discovery that no factor influences the sense of joy in life more than living in accordance with our spiritual gifts. I have seen this at work in my own life. Ever since I consistently began to shape my ministry in harmony with my gifting—which includes refusing to assume responsibilities outside of it— I have experienced three results: first, I am happier; second, I am more effective; and third, I am more misunderstood by fellow Christians than ever before. Many of us are so accustomed to the "square wheel" model that we consider it almost unspiritual for someone to choose to function as a "round wheel."

Wisdom, commitment, power

In my book, *The 3 Colors of Ministry,* I have placed the terms wisdom (for the green area), commitment (for red), and power (for blue) at the center. In any given church you can frequently find one or even two of these dimensions, but a "radical balance" (pages 54-57) of all three dimensions is relatively scarce. There are churches that are quite strong in wisdom, but are lacking both commitment and power. Others might be strong in commitment, but since they are lacking power and wisdom they are not nearly as effective as they could be. Others are

My experiences:

When a Pentecostal church in the United States did its first NCD Survey, gift-based ministry was identified as their lowest factor. Due to their theology that strongly emphasizes spiritual gifts ("If any church knows something about gifts, it's us"), they had difficulty accepting the results. It took some time before they discovered their two root problems. (1) Their perspective was reduced to just a handful of gifts. (2) Only a limited number of people actually practiced their gifts. Changing that paradigm created conflicts, and within the first year the church even lost members. After two years, however, they started to experience the fruit of inner-church reformation.

The secret of gift-based ministry is (a) to grow in each of the areas of wisdom, commitment, and power, and (b) to bring these three dimensions into balance.

already strong in power, but since they are lacking commitment and wisdom, with all of their power they are in danger of doing more harm than good. However, when all three dimensions are in balance, a church functions according to God's design.

Your personal contribution

If you haven't identified your gifts already, do it immediately. Among other things, the book, *The 3 Colors of Ministry,* contains a *Three-Color Gift-Test* that will help you identify which gifts you have, and which you don't have. Does your church involvement match your gifting? If not, don't give up until you find a task that challenges you to grow in the use of your gifts. If necessary, ask your leaders to create gift-based tasks for you.

If you are a leader, one of your major responsibilities is to facilitate this process in your area of responsibility, be it a small group, a local church, or a denomination. Offer gift-counseling. Recruit gift counselors. Develop the habit of speaking about your gifts and your limitations. Refuse to take over responsibilities outside your area of gifting. Model a gift-based approach.

What has been the most inspiring case study of gift-based ministry that you have encountered?

Quality characteristic 3: Passionate spirituality

Chapter 3

The name of this quality characteristic may strike you as a bit abstract, but that is due to the principle-oriented approach. We had to find a term that would describe the most divergent styles of spirituality. As far as church growth is concerned, our research indicates that the important thing is not a church's style, but the degree to which faith is actually lived out with commitment, passion, and enthusiasm. This is what sets growing churches apart from non-growing ones.

> **When it comes to spirituality, evidence that we are growing is more important than our current state.**

Choking spiritual passion

There is one discipline in which Christians have achieved a depressing success: We have invented countless strategies for destroying spiritual passion. In my office I have two hanging files set aside for this quality characteristic. In one file, I collect all the resources I can find that support Christians in living out their spiritual passion more and more consistently. In the second file, I collect concepts that result in choking spiritual passion from the outset. Every time I return from a trip I file the new discoveries I have made in one of those two folders.

My experiences:

When our Korean NCD Partners analyzed the data of all of the churches that had done the NCD Survey, they came up with a surprising discovery. The most frequent minimum factor was passionate spirituality. That was a huge contrast to the widespread notion that many people have about Korean churches, which have set worldwide standards for what passionate spirituality is all about. However, our partners discovered that in the past few years, many churches have put too much pressure on their people. Many have been burned out. Legalistic tendencies have grown. This discovery helped them to encourage an approach to spirituality that seeks to bring the two poles of giving and receiving into a more healthy balance.

Here is the frustrating result: While the first file is not more than an inch wide, the second file has quickly become so full that I cannot close the file drawer anymore. I think that this alone says more about our approach to spiritual passion than most of us are willing to admit.

When analyzing the data of thousands of churches, we made an interesting discovery. The time that people spend in prayer has only a minor correlation to the quality of the church and its growth. However, whether or not prayer is viewed as an "inspiring experience" has a significant relationship to the quality and quantity of the church. We found similar results with respect to the personal use of the Bible and other factors affecting personal spirituality. The quantity is not the decisive factor, but the quality is!

Word-based, Spirit-directed, world-focused

The secret to passionate spirituality is to bring all three colors into balance. We need to cultivate a form of spirituality that is truly based on the Word of God (red area), directed by the Holy Spirit (blue area), and focused on the world (green area). Please notice that this does not imply any compromise between the three areas, which would lead to apathy. Rather, the secret is to strive for a radical development in all three directions: fully Bible-centered, fully Spirit-filled, fully "worldly."

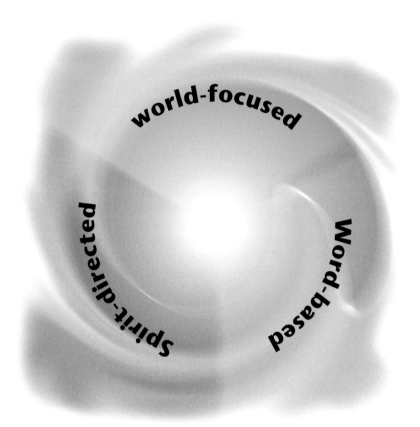

The secret of passionate spirituality is (a) to develop a threefold orientation of being based on the Word, directed by the Spirit, and focused on the world, and (b) to bring these three dimensions into balance.

Your personal contribution

Whenever you encounter simplistic suggestions such as, "Pray more! Read the Bible more often!" etc., be skeptical. While those suggestions may be helpful for some believers, they can be counterproductive for others. Take the three dimensions described above as a starting point. At present, which one is least developed in your life? Is it the red area? Then it may, indeed, be a good suggestion to spend more time in the Word. Or do you feel that your life is not really directed by the Holy Spirit (blue area)? Look for the help of Christians who are more experienced in this area than you are. Or does your spirituality lack a focus on the world? Then most likely you won't be helped by simply praying more. Network with believers who are known for a truly "earthly" kind of spirituality.

Most importantly, strive for continuous growth. Every year, evaluate to what degree you have made progress. There may be years with no progress at all. Acknowledge this; don't regard it as a catastrophe, but as a stimulus. The essence of the Christian faith is to be involved in a constant process of spiritual growth. Evidence that you are growing is more important than your current state.

What has been the most inspiring case study of passionate spirituality that you have encountered?

Quality characteristic 4: Effective structures

Chapter 3

Interestingly enough, of all of the eight quality characteristics, effective structures has emerged as the most controversial. At first sight, this observation doesn't seem to make any sense. How could anyone be interested in ineffective structures? The sad truth is that, in many churches, the model of the cart with the square wheels (page 85) has become so normal that the use of square wheels is even seen as superior to the use of round wheels. I have studied long theological essays that have had no other purpose than to defend a "square-wheel" approach.

> As a leader, take full responsibility for the structures as they are today.

A means to an end

Unfortunately, many people confuse the (constantly changeable) structures of the church with its (unchangeable) essence. Therefore, they are not able to view structures as means to an end. Rather, they strive to maintain the structures as they have always been. For them, the criterion of "effectiveness" is not a spiritual criterion at all. They overlook Scripture's strong warnings against legalistic forms of dealing with structures and its repeated teaching of the criterion of usefulness: "All things are lawful, but not all things are useful. All things are lawful, but not all things edify" (1 Cor. 10:23).

The most important criterion for church structures is the degree to which they fulfill their purpose. Whatever doesn't measure up to this requirement (e.g. demeaning leadership patterns, inconvenient worship service times, or programs that are not effectively reaching their intended audience) should be changed or laid to rest. Through this process of constant renewal, traditionalistic ruts can be avoided to a large extent.

My experiences:

Recently, I had the privilege of attending the worship service of an Australian church that had one of the highest quality results of all churches surveyed in that country. Not surprisingly, it was a relatively small church with 80 people in attendance. They had implemented the NCD principles so consistently that they not only structured the church according to the eight quality characteristics (one leader for each area), but also assigned the names that we use in NCD to each of the areas. Thus, I was introduced to the leaders of loving relationships, holistic small groups, inspiring worship service, etc. These terms seemed to be as natural to them as the terms bishop, diocese, or synod are for members of other churches.

Upward, inward, outward

Whenever I speak on the topic of effective structures, there are people who want me to show a ready-made organizational chart that they can simply take over. However, such a structure doesn't exist. Every church has to develop their own effective structures that fit their specific goals, the size of their church, their history, and their denominational identity.

It is extremely helpful to take the three-color diagram on page 113 as a starting point for analyzing the existing structures. Are they primarily focused on upward, inward, or outward growth? In other words, do they help people experience God (upward dimension), do they strengthen the fellowship of the believers (inward dimension), or are they focused on ministering to the world (outward dimension)? When you do such an analysis, you will quickly find out which areas your church should focus on. It's one thing to verbally affirm that a specific dimension

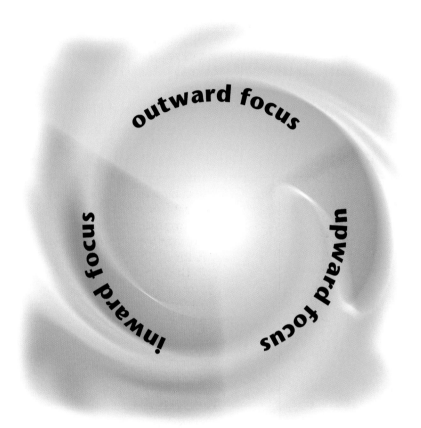

The secret of effective structures is (a) to address each of the three directions (upward, inward, and outward growth) and (b) to bring these three dimensions into balance.

is "important," but it is another thing to develop structures that are targeted on facilitating the development of that specific area.

Your personal contribution

If you are a leader in the church, the most important thing you can do is take full responsibility for the structures as they are today. Never pass this responsibility off to someone else, neither to preceding generations nor to God. Second, evaluate the degree to which each structure fufills its purpose. Third, ask yourself if the structures that do fulfill their purpose are equally directed on the three dimensions mentioned above.

It may be that you aren't in any leadership position that would enable you to change structures directly. If this is so, please, don't make the mistake of taking ineffective structures as a given. Because millions of other believers have made this mistake, the "square-wheels" approach has flourished. If the structures around you are hindering growth, persistently ask your leaders when these structures will be changed. Don't ask *if*, ask *when*. Become pushy in asking this question. And don't forget to make your own powerful contribution to effective structures: Relate your spiritual gifts to concrete tasks in your church.

What has been the most inspiring case study of effective structures that you have encountered?

Quality characteristic 5: Inspiring worship service

There is probably no other area in which the distinction between models and principles (pages 20-22) is so frequently violated as this one. Countless Christians believe that they must adopt particular worship models from other churches, being convinced that these models represent universal principles of growth.

Attending an inspiring worship service is fun.

My experiences:

An African pastor shared with me how his church addressed its minimum factor, inspiring worship service. In their church of about 30 people, they tried to imitate the worship style of model churches with a thousand or more people. As a result, they invested a lot of energy into the worship services and were deeply disappointed when they received the results of the NCD Survey. A detailed analysis of the survey helped them understand that they were following a procedure that didn't fit who they were. In fact, they drastically reduced the energy investment in the worship service and applied a far more informal, family-like, style. Not only did this result in a dramatic quality increase in the area of inspiring worship service (+21), but the quality characteristic of need-oriented evangelism grew by 18 points as well.

One principle—thousands of models and styles

Our research indicates that the question is not whether a worship service targets believers or non-believers; whether it is loaded with Christian symbolism or strives to radiate a secular, business-like atmosphere; whether the worship follows a formal or a more free-flowing style. The key criterion is something else: Is the worship service an inspiring experience for those who attend? It is this aspect that clearly distinguishes growing churches from non-growing ones. And since different people experience different forms of worship as "inspiring," there is no right or wrong when it comes to the various models of worship services. We need different churches with different styles to minister to the large mosaic of different people that makes up today's world.

People who attend inspiring worship services declare that the worship service is—and for some believers this is almost a heretical word—"fun." It is evident that the opposition to this quality characteristic comes from Christians who attend church to fulfill a spiritual duty. They don't attend because it is a wonderful experience that they would not miss for the world, but to do God (or the pastor) a favor. Some even believe that their "faithfulness" in patiently enduring an unpleasant experience is blessed by God. When I share the illustration of the cart with square wheels (page 85) with groups that are conditioned by such thinking, they usually do not see anything humorous in it. For them, to do what the two men in the illustration are doing is something that is absolutely normal, maybe even spiritual. Can you see the connection?

Liturgy, teaching, praise

The forms of worship services in healthy churches can be extremely different, and yet there is a common denominator. In growing churches you will find high quality in the three areas of liturgy (green), teaching (red), and praise (blue).

When considering these areas, note that different groups assign very different meanings to these terms. The term "liturgy," for instance, does not only relate to a "formal style," but "liturgies" can be clearly detected in the midst of a declared "non-liturgi-

The secret of inspiring worship services is (a) to constantly improve the quality in each of the areas of liturgy, teaching, and praise, and (b) to bring these three dimensions into balance.

cal" church. The same applies to the term "praise." It can be practiced in countless different ways, with an organ or a tambourine, with a choir or a band, with clapping or folded hands, with arms lifted up or heads bowed down. Whatever a church's style may be, the secret to health is that all three areas display a high quality and are brought into balance.

Your personal contribution

Maybe you are among those Christians who have believed that enduring a boring worship service is a Christian virtue. You don't have to believe that any longer. You can rightly expect a worship service to be inspiring for you—one that you don't want to miss because it energizes you for the whole week.

On the other hand, it may be that in the past you have encountered God primarily in only one (or two) of the three color areas mentioned above. If this is so, deliberately strive to appreciate the color areas that have not meant anything to you yet. It is not only the church's responsibility to strive to bring balance to the worship services, but it is also the responsibility of each individual believer to seek a more holistic experience of God in worship as well.

What has been the most inspiring case study of inspiring worship services that you have encountered?

Quality characteristic 6: Holistic small groups

A balanced small group nurtures the heads, the hands, and the hearts of its participants.

My experiences:

When I did a seminar in Northern Norway, far above the arctic circle, some participants told me that the concept of holistic small groups didn't really fit their culture, as people aren't accustomed to sharing personal things with others. One of the pastors reported that this had been his impression as well when his church identified holistic small groups as their minimum factor. After 17 months, however, holistic small groups had become their new maximum factor. What had they done? "I had to train people to share about their personal lives," the pastor said. "Whenever I met a church member I would ask: Have you experienced anything meaningful that you would like to share with me?" After a while, people started to love this question and to ask it themselves.

Growing churches have developed a system of small groups where individual believers can find intimate community, practical help, and intense spiritual interaction. In these groups, people not only discuss biblical texts and listen to their leader's interesting explanations, but they apply biblical insights to the questions the participants have about everyday life issues.

Ruling out anonymity

In one of my seminars I shared the story of the world's largest church in Seoul, Korea, which at that time had half a million members. One of the participants immediately responded that she could not even imagine becoming part of such a church. When I asked her why she felt that way, she said, "Well, I could never stand the anonymity. I need the familiar atmosphere of people I know well." Just a short time later I met a pastor from that church and asked him how they dealt with the problem of anonymity. He looked rather puzzled. "Anonymity?", he asked. "Nobody has ever complained about that in our church." He told me how their church has developed a network of cell groups with no more than twelve members in which most of the church members are involved.

I am well aware that managing the specific problems of the world's largest church is very likely not your primary concern. However, our research shows that the principle on which this Korean church is based has universal validity. Christian small groups are not a nice, yet dispensable, hobby. No, it's the very essence of the church of Jesus Christ to provide places where believers can find this kind of intimate community.

Heads, hands, hearts

The best way to understand what holistic small groups are is to see them as a "church in microcosm." That means you can expect everything that characterizes the church as a whole—for instance, the eight quality characteristics—to function, with slight variations, at the small group level as well. Holistic small groups should nurture the heads (green area), hands (red), and hearts (blue) of the participants. If just one of these dimensions is missing or underdeveloped, it might still be a small group that fulfills an important function, but it is no longer a "holistic" small group.

Your personal contribution

If you are in a leadership position for the whole church, analyze the small groups of the church in terms of how holistically they function. If you are a small group leader, focus on your own group. Does it effectively address the heads, hands,

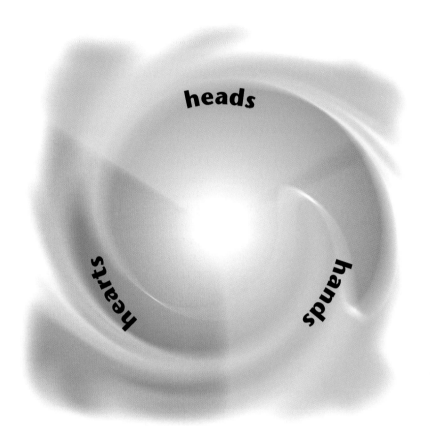

The secret of holistic small groups is (a) to nurture the heads, the hands, and the hearts of the participants, and (b) to bring these three dimensions into balance.

and hearts of its participants? Does one of these three areas need your special attention?

Finally, if you are a member of a small group that doesn't function as holistically as it should, there is good news for you. This is the area of church life where you have the greatest opportunity to bring about dramatic changes without holding an official leadership position. Since small groups depend on the personal involvement of its members, every member has a direct impact on how holistic the group is. Growing in the three areas mentioned is often not so much a programmatic decision, but rather a result of each individual members' participation in the group.

Let's assume, for example, that the blue segment is underdeveloped in your group. Your contribution could be to make deliberate efforts to share from your heart. If red is underdeveloped, encourage others to participate in corporate activities. If green should be your minimum factor, stimulate the group with arguments and facts. Since small groups play such an essential role as a "church in microcosm," we have developed the majority of our NCD tools for use at the small group level. This is where transformational learning (pages 41-43) is easiest to achieve.

What has been the most inspiring case study of holistic small groups that you have encountered?

Quality characteristic 7: Need-oriented evangelism

I t certainly doesn't take a worldwide research project to convince people that church growth is inconceivable without evangelism. How else could the church grow if not through the process of sharing the gospel to bring more and more people into the body of Christ? This process is generally called "evangelism."

A secret of healthy churches is to meet the needs of non-Christians.

My experiences:

Need-oriented evangelism works best if a church ranks high in loving relationships. This has been the experience of a church in Malaysia that focused, for one year, on loving relationships. At the end of that year, the NCD Survey revealed that the quality in loving relationships had increased by 20 points, and that the new minimum factor was need-oriented evangelism. Based on their previous experiences, they initiated highly creative, need-meeting events, including free medical tests for senior citizens and badminton championships. People experienced these evangelistic activities as expressions of God's love.

The decisive ingredient

Therefore, the exciting question in our research was not to explore whether or not evangelism was necessary, but to identify the decisive ingredient in the evangelistic outreach of growing churches. There are some people who feel evangelism works best when you push people to commit their lives to Christ. Some don't even shy away from manipulative methods to reach this goal. Since this image of "effective evangelism" is so widespread, it is no wonder that many Christians feel a strange sensation in their stomach when they hear the word "evangelism." Of course, they want people to find a personal relationship with Christ. But what they don't want is to copy these pushy methods that have been inseparably connected to the term "evangelism."

However, it can be shown that pushy, manipulative methods represent the exact opposite of the practice we learn from growing churches. Their secret is to share the gospel in a way that answers the questions and meets the needs of non-believers.

Pray, care, share

The "lighthouse movement" has coined the terminology "pray, care, share" for their approach to evangelism. I couldn't imagine a more fitting description of how need-oriented evangelism manifests itself in practical terms. When you observe Christianity in a given country or denomination, you can be sure to find each of these three components somewhere: Some groups focus on the blue segment (stressing prayer and the supernatural dimension), others focus on the green segment (stressing caring for people and ministering to their needs), and others on the red segment (sharing the gospel). It is seldom that all three of these dimensions come together in one place. However, that is the key. Can you imagine how powerful evangelism would be if all three dimensions were strongly developed and strategically related to each other?

I don't have to imagine this, since I have seen the results of that approach again and again. People sense that they are literally drawn to Jesus by an invisible power. At the moment they are exposed to the message of the gospel (red area), it

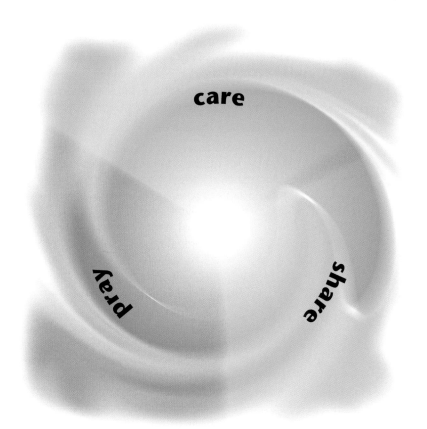

care

pray

share

The secret of need-oriented evangelism is (a) to grow in each of the areas of prayer, caring, and sharing, and (b) to bring these three dimensions into balance.

immediately makes sense to them because they have already experienced the power of the gospel through the prayer (blue area) and the care (green area) of the Christian community.

Your personal contribution

As NCD is a gift-based approach (quality characteristic 2), we don't teach that "every believer is an evangelist." Rather, there are Christians who have that gift, and there are others who don't. But all of us are responsible for fulfilling the Great Commission by investing our specific gifts into the area of evangelism.

This is where the Trinitarian Compass becomes so powerful. In each of the three color areas, a plethora of different gifts is needed to make evangelism effective. Without a doubt, the gift of evangelism plays a central role particularly in the red area with its focus on sharing the gospel. But whether you have the gift of helps, organization, prayer, counseling, artistic creativity, voluntary poverty, or any other gifts that the Scriptures mention, your gifts are urgently needed. Need-oriented evangelism can only take place when everyone in the body of Christ is investing his or her individual gifts in all three areas.

What has been the most inspiring case study of need-oriented evangelism that you have encountered?

Quality characteristic 8: Loving relationships

Chapter 3

Whether you like the term or not, it can be demonstrated that growing churches display a higher "love quotient" than stagnant or declining ones. Whenever I use this term at a conference there are a few Christians who can't stand it: "What a terrible expression!" I can imagine that you might feel the same way. So let me explain what we did in order to measure this "love quotient."

What the NCD Survey measures

The NCD Survey contains a number of questions that enable us to determine how loving the relationships between church members are. For instance, we ask how much time members spend with one another outside of official, church-sponsored events. How often do they invite one another for meals or a cup of coffee? How generous is the church in doling out compliments? To what extent is the pastor aware of the personal needs of the church's lay people? How much laughter is there in the church?

Authentic love makes a church magnetically attractive.

What were the results? All of these points—and quite a few more—have a strong correlation with the growth of the church. In fact, factors like these turned out to be statistically more significant than many of the methods that a number of books have elevated to the status of church growth principles. Is this really so surprising? Authentic love endows a church with a much greater magnetic power than all the marketing efforts in the world. At best, marketing the church can be compared to artificial flowers: they may look real, but they have no fragrance. Real love, however, spreads that mysterious scent that few can resist.

Justice, truth, grace

What are the ingredients of love according to Scripture? In my book, *The 3 Colors of Love,* I have shown that the biblical concept is based on the three pillars of justice (green segment), truth (red), and grace (blue) and that the challenge is to bring these three dimensions into balance.

Far more widespread than the biblical concept, however, is the secular-romantic notion of love that almost completely eliminates justice and truth and reduces grace to only certain aspects of the biblical understanding of grace. Since this use of language has influenced Christianity as well, striving for a balance of justice, truth, and grace is regarded by many people as a "new" approach, overlooking the fact that it is as old as the Old Testament. By identifying which of these aspects is currently least developed, a church can get a helpful indication of which area it should focus on.

My experiences:

When doing a conference in Costa Rica, a pastor complained that the NCD Survey had revealed a "wrong result." Their minimum factor had been loving relationships. "But actually," he told me, "we are quite strong in that area." When we went through the criteria that constitute this quality characteristic, we found out that their notion was almost exclusively shaped by a secular-romantic concept of love, rather than an attempt to bring justice, truth, and grace into balance. I have seen this common tendency in many Latin American churches.

The secret of loving relationships is (a) to develop each of the areas of justice, truth, and grace, and (b) to bring these three dimensions into balance.

Your personal contribution

Ask yourself how strongly developed each of the three dimensions of love are in your life. The book, *The 3 Colors of Love,* provides a scientific test to help you identify that area. The test results will help you (a) to invest your strengths more consistently into church development, and (b) to focus your growth path on the area that is presently least developed in your life. By increasing the quality in that area, you will be able to reflect God's love more completely than you do now, both inside and outside of your church involvements.

Growing in love works best when it is tackled within the context of a group of fellow believers. The ideal place is a small group. The wonderful thing about such a corporate undertaking is that it enables you to network with people who have strengths in those color segments that are currently less developed in your life, and who have weaknesses in areas where you are strong. This kind of give and take—teaching and being taught, admonishing and encouraging, giving and receiving—is an impressive demonstration of what Christian community is all about.

What has been the most inspiring case study of loving relationships that you have encountered?

How to apply these principles

W ho is responsible for applying the principles described in this chapter? There are two answers. First, it is primarily the responsibility of the church leadership; second, it is the responsibility of every individual believer. Let's take a closer look at these two assertions.

The responsibility of the leaders

I have met many leaders who don't see it as part of their responsibility to relate these principles to the daily lives of their churches. When they deal with a church situation that is less than ideal—and that is the starting point in *any* church—they tend to pass the responsibility off to someone or something else: the spirit of the times, the traditions of the church, the unwillingness of the people, the expectations of the denomination, the decisions of past generations. Without a doubt, there is always more than a grain of truth in these answers, but they must never serve as an excuse for not taking responsibility and doing one's best to take the next steps to greater health.

> Only after careful diagnosis will you know which medicine to take.

While discussing the extremely ineffective structures in his local church, a Lutheran pastor in Germany told me, "God is the only one responsible for these structures. We just have to accept them as they are." I replied, "There are many individuals responsible for these structures, but God is definitely not one of them. I can assure you that he never created ineffective structures. We human beings did. It may be that some of these structures were designed by other people a long time ago. But they are no longer responsible for them, we are. As leaders, it is definitely not our task to accept the structures as they are, but to strive for change. That is what God expects of leaders. If we fail to do so, we are unfaithful. And that, according to Scripture, is a serious situation." I find the tendency to shift responsibility to others—especially if it is shifted to God—extremely troublesome. When dealing with such a situation, I have repeatedly opened the first pages of the Bible, read the story of Adam and Eve and the serpent, and asked the respective leaders if that story has, in any way, spoken to them. Some have understood immediately, some have not had the slightest idea what I was driving at.

More on the web:

On the internet (see page 162) you will find answers to the following questions:

• *Do all growing churches display high quality?*

• *What can be done if the church leadership is not open to NCD?*

I have to add, however, that the overwhelming majority of leaders I have met are ready to take responsibility. They are well aware that this is a challenging task, but one that God both expects and empowers them to fulfill.

The responsibility of every Christian

It would be a gross misunderstanding to see church development as a topic primarily for leaders. I hope that the past few pages have shown

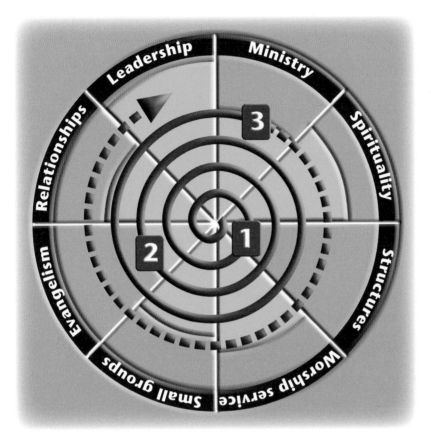

The relationship between qualitative (yellow slices) and quantitative growth (spiral) in a church: According to NCD, the quality of the church in all eight areas determines the evolution of worship service attendance (quantity). The weakest quality characteristic (minimum factor) plays the critical role.

how every Christian can apply the principles of church development in his or her area of influence and thus contribute to the health of the church. Since healthy churches are growing churches, as our research has revealed, your contribution to church health is, at the same time, an effective contribution to church growth.

What is the greatest need in your church?

When being exposed to the NCD principles for the first time, some people sigh, "And I am supposed to apply all of this at the same time? I cannot see the forest for the trees."

The good news is that you don't have to apply everything at the same time. To begin with, it is sufficient to focus on one single area. Which area is the most strategic and crucial area? Here the so-called "minimum factor" plays a critical role. The next chapter deals with the role that the minimum factor plays in your personal life, in your local church, in your denomination, and even in your whole country. It is important to identify that factor, as only after a careful diagnosis will you know which medicine to take.

How open is your church to applying the principles of NCD? What might be obstacles?

The Minimum Factor

4

What's the deciding factor when it comes to seeking personal growth and the growth of your church? Most people believe that it is difficult to narrow down the answer to this question. Without a doubt, there are many areas of the Christian life that are difficult to tackle—understanding the Bible, growing in love, dealing with conflicts, to name just a few. There are, however, other tasks that are not difficult at all. Discovering the key factor for growth falls into this category. In Natural Church Development, we call it the "minimum factor."

Chapter 4

Where the minimum factor applies—and where it doesn't

I n your quest to experience growth, should you focus on your strengths or on your weaknesses? I am aware that there are serious Christians who have a standard answer to this question on hand, such as, "Always focus on your strength," or "Always focus on your weakness." In this chapter I want to show you how such an answer can be misleading.

The truth is that there are areas in which you should focus on your greatest strengths, and there are other areas in which you should address your weaknesses. Using our NCD terminology, the first approach could be described as a "maximum factor approach," while the second one would be a "minimum factor approach."

Minimum and maximum factors

Reflect on this for a moment. When Scripture speaks about spiritual gifts (in Romans 12 or 1 Corinthians 12, for instance), does it reveal a maximum or a minimum factor approach? It's definitely a maximum factor approach. The basic message is this: Focus on the gifts that God has given you, and let other Christians practice other gifts. However, when Paul, in Galatians 5, speaks about the "Fruit of the Spirit," a minimum factor approach applies. If the fruit of joy is already well-developed in your life, but you lack self-discipline, you should not say: "I will continue to radiate joy and let other Christians practice self-discipline." No, in this case you must deliberately focus your attention on developing your personal minimum factor: self-discipline.

So, how do you know whether to apply the minimum or the maximum factor approach? It is really not that difficult to distinguish between them. Whenever you deal with essential health factors—features that are absolutely necessary for the functioning of the organism—the minimum factor approach applies. For instance, if you are lacking vitamin C, you cannot say, "I will compensate with more vitamin A." No, you need to focus on your "minimum vitamin" in order to restore your health. When you are dealing with non-essential factors, however, the maximum factor approach tends to be more productive. For example, if you are considering which kind of fruit you would like to eat (oranges, apples, or mangoes), you can simply choose what you like best, since all of them contain vitamin C.

Minimum and maximum approaches in the church

The same applies to the church. As long as you are dealing with absolutely essential elements, you have to focus on your

> The minimum factor approach helps you focus your attention on the most strategic areas.

My experiences:

Identifying a minimum factor does not necessarily imply that the church is weak in that area. Every church—even the best in the world—has one area that ranks lower than the other ones. The church with the highest NCD scores worldwide is a 300-member church in Korea. Their average score is 98.5, and their minimum factor is empowering leadership with a score of 84. In other words, the quality characteristic empowering leadership is extremely well developed in that church and can even serve as a model for other churches. Yet it is still the area that the church should focus on.

50
40
30
20
10
0

Leadership Ministry Spirituality Structures Worship service Small groups Evangelism Relationships

This is the profile of a church in Great Britain. Their minimum factor is passionate spirituality; their maximum factor, effective structures. This church should focus on its spirituality in order to progress. Further improvement of its structures would not solve the root problem.

minimum factor; when you are dealing with areas in which you have different, equally valid options, focus on the maximum factor. In other words, when it comes to principles of church health, apply the minimum factor approach. When it comes to non-essential questions such as the kind of music to use at a Christian meeting, please, do God and the congregation a favor and apply the maximum factor approach!

The minimum factor in NCD

There are two major areas in NCD where the minimum factor approach plays a significant role:

1. The **eight quality characteristics** of healthy churches, because every single factor is absolutely essential for the health of the church.

2. The **three colors approach**, because each color symbolizes an indispensable biblical dimension.

This chapter will show you how to apply the minimum factor approach to both areas. In order to achieve balance and to restore health, you need to focus your attention on your weakest areas. While all of the eight quality characteristics and all of the three colors are *equally* important from an objective point of view, there is always one area that is *more* important than the others at the present time. The minimum factor approach helps you focus your attention on that crucial area.

More on the web:

On the internet (see page 162) you will find answers to the following questions:

- *Which research results back up the minimum factor approach?*

- *What difference does it make whether the minimum factor is on a high or on a low level?*

Based on your intuition, what would you see as the minimum factor of your church?

Chapter 4

Learning from a potted plant

As many of NCD's building blocks, the minimum factor approach has been inspired by models from nature. Our Australian NCD partners like to use the analogy of a potted plant to illustrate these dynamics (see diagrams on page 129).

Four factors that influence growth

A potted plant owes its growth to four factors: nutrients, water, location, and the size of the pot. As long as the ideal conditions are provided by all four elements, growth takes place *all by itself*. Growth is hindered, however, as soon as one of the factors is no longer sufficient enough to support the development of the plant.

For example, if the plant lacks water, its growth will be hindered (diagram 1). Should this deficiency be overcome by watering the plant, it will continue to grow until another factor becomes the new minimum factor, for instance, the size of the pot (diagram 2). If, at that point, more water is added to prompt further growth—a procedure that had been so successful in the past—what previously was a deficiency would now become an excess (diagram 3), and the surplus of water would actually harm the plant. The moment you focus on the new minimum factor, however, growth will be stimulated again (diagram 4).

The blessings of water

These dynamics explain two phenomena that can frequently be observed in church development:

1. The same measure that has brought about growth in the past may actually hinder growth later on.

2. The same measure that one church applies with great success has counterproductive effects in other churches.

Let's assume your church has experienced how strongly God has used "water" to facilitate growth. Just by adding this one element, you could almost double your worship attendance. Without a doubt, such an experience will have a lasting impact. All of a sudden, you will begin to read Scripture through new eyes. Doesn't the Bible start with the statement that the Spirit of God was "hovering over the waters" (Gen. 1:2)? And isn't it the final promise of the Bible that we will receive the "free gift of the water of life" (Rev. 22:17)? Doesn't Psalm 23 promise that God will lead us to "quiet waters" to restore our souls? Doesn't Isaiah clearly say, "I will pour water on the thirsty land" (Isa. 44:3)? Didn't Jesus himself speak about "streams of living water" (John 7:38)? Some will even recall that Jesus walked on water and transformed water into wine. Based on all of that, you might wish to develop a "water church" and sponsor nationwide "water conferences" to teach others how to experience the same blessings as you did.

Water is good for a plant, but more water is not necessarily better.

My experiences:

The potted plant analogy teaches you to constantly shift your focus rather than continue with what has been successful in the past. The very things that might have brought a blessing to your church two years ago could be counterproductive today. My experience has been that many Christians have great difficulty following this line of thinking. If they have once experienced God at work through a certain measure, they tend to see it as a cure-for-all-problems for the rest of their lives. The potted plant analogy can help overcome that kind of thinking.

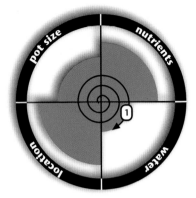

Diagram 1: While three of the four essential factors (nutrients, location, pot size) provide ideal conditions, growth is hindered by insufficient water.

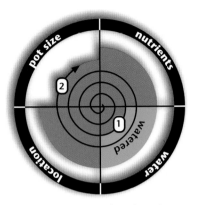

Diagram 2: Once the plant has been sufficiently watered, growth continues until it is slowed down by insufficient pot size.

The analogy of the potted plant helps us understand complicated dynamics of church development in an easy-to-grasp way. It draws our attention to the crucial questions of timing and a consistent focus on the key obstacles to ongoing growth.

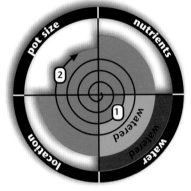

Diagram 3: Should you follow your past experience and increase your watering, having experienced such positive results in the past, you will harm the plant. At this point, the growth is limited by the pot size, not by insufficient water.

Diagram 4: The moment you address the new minimum factor (pot size), growth will continue until it is stopped by a new minimum factor (location).

Hopefully, it is self-evident that this procedure will not work. It will actually do more harm than good. Rather than experiencing "streams of living water," people will drown. And five years later, the term "water" will be banned, because everybody has experienced its catastrophic effects. So, were you wrong in assuming that water is such a great gift? No, that assumption was correct. You simply failed to regard the dynamics that can be learned from the growth of the potted plant.

Are you aware of any church programs that worked at one time, but not at other times?

Chapter 4

The image of the minimum barrel

Ⅰf the minimum factor plays such a crucial role in church develop-ment, the question becomes how to communicate this truth in a way that will have a lasting impact on people.

The weakest element determines the success of the whole enterprise.

My experiences:

When I did an NCD conference in Indonesia, countless churches had just experienced a revival with quite dramatic growth. However, in the midst of this revival, many churches had not experienced any growth at all. I asked one of the pastors how he would explain this phe-nomenon. "Brother Christian, you should know that better than I," he said and showed me the picture of the minimum barrel. "Those churches that are now experiencing such dra-matic growth, have diligently and consistently worked on the quality of their minimum barrel for years. Now God is pouring water out on all of the churches, but only those with high enough staves are able to contain it. That is why some are so dramatically affected by the revival and others, not at all."

A live demonstration

The best way that I can think of is to expose people to a small live demonstration. Based on the picture on page 131, a friend of mine has built a minimum barrel that I can use in my seminars. This barrel is basically nothing more than a tub with staves of varying lengths. When I visit a church that has conducted an NCD Survey, I write the names of the eight quality characteristics on the staves according to how strongly or weakly each of the individual characteristics is developed. The name of the minimum factor is written on the shortest stave (for instance, effective structures) and the name of the maximum factor, on the longest (for instance, inspiring worship service).

Then I pour water into the barrel until it starts to overflow. While I am pouring and the feet of those sitting in the front row are getting wet, I ask the participants what I should do. At that point, a number of people demand that I immedi-ately stop pouring the water. I don't, of course, because in this demonstration the water symbolizes God's blessing flow-ing down from heaven into the church. We cannot seriously want to ask God to stop pouring out his blessing just because our church has trouble holding the water.

Others might suggest that we should pray more. I agree that prayer is extremely important and absolutely essential for church growth, so I extend the stave with the term "pas-sionate spirituality," which is already quite long, four more inches, and everyone can see that this noble measure doesn't solve the problem. The water still keeps splashing down onto the floor. Eventually someone (most likely, the facilities man-ager) suggests that I should lengthen the minimum factor stave, "effective structures." And look at that! As soon as I lengthen it just one inch, the barrel can hold one more inch of water.

God's responsibility and our responsibility

Such a demonstration illustrates well the central issues in church development. The different staves of the barrel (qual-ity characteristics) represent what we can and, according to God's will, should do. However, our industrious improve-ments in the quality of the barrel cannot cause the water (newly won people) to flow into it. If God doesn't fill it, even

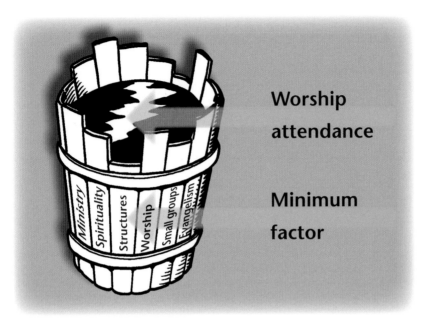

Worship

attendance

Minimum

factor

The staves of this minimum barrel represent church quality and the water represents quantity. This illustrates the significance of the minimum factor approach to church development.

the finest barrel will stay empty. On the other hand, if God does pour water out—and there is much theological evidence that he really likes to do that—then the quality of our barrel (church) is the deciding factor, as it determines how much water (people) the barrel can hold.

Many Christians confuse these two dimensions. They believe that they are responsible for bringing about numerical growth. At the same time, they neglect their responsibility for the quality of the church in the eight areas. Then, when God actually pours water down from heaven, their churches are simply not prepared to receive that blessing.

The limitations of analogies

Of course, just as with biblical parables, we must not confuse the literal and figurative meanings of such an illustration. At some point, every analogy breaks down. However, as long as we remember not to stretch the point, these object lessons are very useful tools for teaching the basics of NCD: the relationship between God's work and ours, between quality and quantity, between improving all eight factors at the same time and the minimum factor in particular.

In one case, a church in which I had done the minimum barrel demonstration wanted to charge me for the restoration of the floor, since I had used colored water which had literally had a "lasting impact." I was not ready to accept the charges. I wrote to them, "I know that you believe in symbols. Take the stain on the floor as a lasting symbol for what can happen if we violate God's principles. That might speak to future generations just as powerfully as the carved angels behind your pulpit."

Do you agree that increasing the quality of the church is our human responsibility?

Application 1: Quality characteristics

If you want to apply the minimum factor approach to the eight quality characteristics, you need an instrument with which you can measure the quality in each of the eight areas. This is what the NCD Survey has been designed to do (more on page 152). In order to develop a church profile, the computer compares the answers of your church members with the 168 million individual responses that have been calculated to date.

The survey is complex from the programmer's point of view, but quite easy to understand from the user's perspective: 30 people fill in a questionnaire, the answers are inserted into a computer program, and the church receives a score for each of the eight quality characteristics that is displayed as a bar graph similar to the diagram on page 133. The value 50 represents the average scores of all of the churches that have already done the NCD Survey in a given country. This means that every score above 50 is above average and every score below 50 is below average. Most importantly, the diagram reveals at a glance what the current minimum factor is.

> The greatest obstacle is that many people simply don't want to be exposed to the truth.

The survey measures the eight adjectives

What exactly does the NCD Survey measure? You may remember (page 105) that each of the eight quality characteristics consists of two parts, an *adjective* (such as, empowering, gift-based, passionate, etc.) and a *noun* (leadership, ministry, spirituality, etc.). What the survey measures is how strongly the adjectives in each of the eight areas are developed.

Take a look at the diagram on page 133. The score 51 for empowering leadership (the first bar) does not express how strong, visionary, autocratic, pastoral, or popular the leadership is. It exclusively expresses how *empowering* it is. The same holds true for the other seven quality characteristics. The score for effective structures, for example, doesn't reveal how many structures there are, whether they are old or new, visible or invisible. It exclusively measures how *effective* they are.

No self-evaluation

It's important to know that the NCD Survey doesn't ask for any "evaluation" of the church, as many people might expect. The survey doesn't contain a single question that would ask, "How empowering is the leadership of your church?", "How effective are the structures?", or "How loving are the relationships?" Answers to these questions would not be at all helpful in assessing the quality of a local church. Instead of asking, "How would you rate the quality of your church on a scale of 1-100?", the majority of the questions are concerned with

My experiences:

I sometimes meet pastors who tell me how they have "measured" the quality of their church without using a scientific survey. Of course, everyone is free to do that. The major reason why I would not recommend such a procedure is that without a scientific normation, there is no standard for comparing the quality in each of the eight areas. Moreover, there is the danger of projecting our own favorite views of the church onto reality and ending up "measuring" them rather than the real situation. To do such a "home-made" analysis is not always without value, as it may stimulate interesting discussion, but it does not substitute for the accuracy of an objective scientific approach such as the NCD Survey.

The NCD Survey draws your attention to the strategic factor for growth. As the latest version of the survey is based on the data of more than 40,000 churches, it provides highly reliable results.

what the person who fills in the questionnaire has actually *experienced* in the past few months.

Resistance to the survey

The benefits of doing the survey are overwhelming. Why is it, then, that some church leaders are against it? The number one reason is that many people simply don't want to be exposed to the truth. To a certain degree, I can understand that. As long as you don't know how healthy or sick you are, you don't have to think about therapy. Just as some people constantly avoid doctors, some Christian leaders flee a congregational health check-up.

Of course, resistance toward the survey can have other roots as well. Churches that have a low view of the "green area" in general, often cannot see any spiritual relevance in doing such an empirical study. The only way to convince them is to expose them to the benefits of regular results, as these are, in every single case, loaded with spiritual impact.

> **More on the web:**
>
> *On the internet (see page 162) you will find answers to the following questions:*
>
> • *Why do only 30 people fill in the NCD Survey?*
>
> • *Are there situations in which the NCD Survey should not be done?*

Regular background activity

In countless churches around the globe, doing the NCD Survey has already become what it was designed to be: a regular background activity to monitor the current health of the church. As NCD is built on universal principles rather than featuring a specific model, style, or theology, the survey can be conducted in any church model. The results of the survey will help you become more effective in applying your specific model of ministry.

Doing the NCD Survey regularly should be a normal background activity of the church.

The benefits of repeated surveys

Natural Church Development does not promote conducting just one survey and contemplating its practical consequences for the rest of one's life. One survey can be eye-opening, of course, but you will only be able to see developments and trends in the eight quality areas if you do this kind of health check regularly. And that is where things really get exciting.

Our recommendation is that you do the survey once a year. That way you will have current data about the qualitative development of your church, which will be of utmost relevance for almost all areas of church leadership. Why should you do such a health check regularly? Here are the most important reasons:

• Once you are involved with the NCD process, the quality in the eight areas will change rather quickly. It is not uncommon for a minimum factor to become the maximum factor after twelve months. Do you remember the potted plant analogy (page 128)? Then you know why it can be counterproductive to continue watering a plant when you should shift your attention to the size of the pot.

• When you address your minimum factor, all of the other quality characteristics are influenced as well, both positively and negatively. It is extremely valuable to explore why this happens.

• Only by doing the survey regularly can you objectively assess whether or not you have made progress. Did you actually grow in loving relationships or not? If you ask ten different people to give their opinions on that question, you might get ten different answers. The survey supplies you with an objectively verifiable answer.

• By doing the survey regularly, you will have a reliable basis for church planning. Which themes should you focus on this year? What kind of training should you offer? What do the small groups need to focus on? Of course, there are a number of other factors that influence these decisions as well, but the information from a current profile can be extremely helpful in setting priorities.

Has your church already done the NCD Survey? If so, how long ago?

• It should be noted that the survey enables you to see even very small progress in a given area (say, an increase of 2 or 3 points). It is encouraging to be able to visualize such small progress that might otherwise be completely overlooked. Doing the survey regularly enables you to celebrate even tiny steps in the right direction.

Application 2: Trinitarian Compass

Chapter 4

The second major area in which the minimum factor approach applies relates to the three colors that serve as symbols for three foundational biblical dimensions. Having already taken the NCD Color Profile (pages 72-79), I am sure you have gained an initial understanding of these dynamics.

Whether you evaluate the results of the Color Profile on a purely personal or on a corporate level (such as your small group or your whole church), you should always focus on the least developed color. Why? Because it's your present minimum factor.

Different tests based on the Trinitarian Compass

Based on the model of the Trinitarian Compass, we have developed a number of tests—and will continue to do so—that address different areas. The NCD Color Profile, for instance, has been designed as a generic test that reveals general tendencies in your life and the life of your church. Each of the books in the *NCD Discipleship Resources* series (page 155) contains a test that relates the Trinitarian Compass to one of the eight quality characteristics. For instance, in the book, *The 3 Colors of Ministry*, the Trinitarian Compass is applied to the area of gift-based ministry; in *The 3 Colors of Love,* you find a test that relates the three colors to the "Fruit of the Spirit," which Paul describes in Galatians 5.

Please keep in mind that you may display different colors in different areas of your life. You might be primarily "green" in the area of evangelism, but "red/blue" in your spiritual gifting. There are very few people who display the same color profile in all areas of their lives. Honestly, I am so glad that reality is like that. In contrast to some Christians who would like to draw strict lines between the three colors, in reality we find all of the colors in every denomination, in every church, in every small group, and even in every believer. It is just in the *ratio* of the individual colors where people and churches differ from one another.

A "radical balance"

When dealing with John's vision of the New Jerusalem (page 56) we saw that a biblical approach to balance does not mean to be "moderate" in all three areas. Such a balance could be achieved by constantly *reducing* the quality of your "maximum color." However, the goal of biblical balance is to increase the quality in all three color segments. Due to this growth process, you will become an increasingly radical Christian. It's true that keeping the colors in balance will help you avoid the dangers that are connected with each individual color (page 58),

The Trinitarian Compass brings focus to the spiritual life of the church members.

More on the web:

On the internet (see page 162) you will find answers to the following questions:

• *Which tests have already been developed by NCD for applying the Trinitarian Compass to various areas?*

• *How often should such a test be repeated in order to monitor one's progress?*

but this does not mean that the radicalness of the three colors will be in any way compromised. The Trinitarian Compass will help you radically apply the green, red, and blue dimensions to your life.

In the previous paragraph, I deliberately used the term "radical" several times in order to discover what kind of emotions this term evokes in you. Be honest, how did you respond when you read that word? Negatively or positively? I you are like most people that I know, you probably experienced primarily negative feelings. "Radical"—when hearing this word, many of us think of extremists, fundamentalists, fanatics, maybe even terrorists, but at the very least people with quite unhealthy, imbalanced views.

Revising our view of radicalness

I want to encourage you to reconsider your definition of the term "radical." Whenever you encounter that term in this book, think of Jesus. He was definitely radical in all aspects of his life. At the same time, he is the best model of spiritual balance. According to Scripture, radicalness and balance are not mutually exclusive concepts. They are two different aspects of the same growth process. The Trinitarian Compass has been designed to bring these two dimensions together.

Why do most of us associate primarily negative things with the term "radical"? Applying the categories of the Trinitarian Compass, this is relatively easy to explain. Most "radical Christians" that you have encountered have probably been radical in one specific color segment. But since they were so imbalanced and ignorant about the other two color segments, their radicalness actually appeared fanatical. As we have repeatedly seen, heresy is not always the opposite of the truth. It can also be a partial truth: declaring one of the three colors as an absolute while ignoring the other two. Encountering this kind of "radical" person can be extremely unpleasant. But people who are radical in all three dimensions at the same time? I can assure you: They're great fun to be around!

Becoming a radical Christian

I would like to encourage you to become a "radical Christian" in the best sense of this word: a person who is firmly connected to the *radix*, the root, of the Christian faith—to Jesus Christ himself; who pursues all the concerns that were important to Jesus (and not just a harmless, politically correct selection of them); who reflects all the colors of God's love. Do you know what will happen as you grow in that way? People will watch you and encounter... Jesus.

> The Trinitarian Compass shows you your direction for further growth.

My experiences:

In the past few years, I have used our various Trinitarian Compass tests with extremely different groups. The wonderful thing about these tools is that they enable us within minutes to speak about very personal experiences. In NCD conferences, I like to do interviews on the platform with participants who have done one of these tests. I cannot recall a single time when this would have resulted in an embarrassing situation—in spite of the fact that the themes covered by the tests are both intimate and controversial. I attribute this to the basic rule of the Trinitarian Compass: Everyone has something to give, and everyone has something to learn. It's simply fun to see this rule in action.

The Trinitarian Compass is a tool that makes it easy to speak about personal spiritual experiences in public. It enables different Christians to learn from each other and to help each other in their growth processes.

I felt it was important to share these personal things with you before continuing to speak about empirical research, minimum factors, church profiles, and universal principles. Remember, the goal of all of these activities is a spiritual one: helping you become transformed into the image that God has in mind for you. As I write these lines, I am praying that God will actually initiate this process in your head, heart, and hands, and that it won't take long before you see the fruit.

A book on church development

I am aware that this is supposed to be a book on church development, not on personal spirituality. Why, then, do I stress the personal dimension so much? It is because this book deals with the secret of growing churches. Very likely, in our institute we have collected more data to answer the question of what makes a church grow than anybody else. Thus, if I address this question, you can be sure that I don't take it lightly. I have invested almost all of my life in providing the best answer possible based on the most comprehensive research that has ever been done on this topic.

What is the secret of growing churches? To set numerical growth goals for your church ("By the end of July we will have 250 more members")? To apply marketing techniques to your PR activities? To copy the experiences of megachurches? To push people to get more involved in outreach? To wait for a revival? Forget all of that! There is not the slightest empirical evidence that any of these things could be the "secret of success." To summarize the secret that we did identify, it is this: believers who strive to reflect all the colors of God's love in their lives, supported by leaders who are doing their best to encourage and stimulate these processes creatively.

How, then, will the church grow if we are no longer thinking about church growth? Once the foundation is laid, growth happens *all by itself.*

According to the NCD Color Profile (page 77), which color segment should you focus on?

Chapter 4

The minimum factor within a minimum factor

O ver the last few pages, you have studied two areas in which the minimum factor approach should be applied: *Quality Character- istics* and *Trinitarian Compass.* From the local church perspective, it is highly rewarding to combine these two dimensions with each other. First, discover which of the eight quality characteristics is your church's present minimum factor. Second, analyze the "color balance" in that area. Each of the books that we are developing to address the different quality characteristics (see page 155), includes a test that can help you conduct such an analysis.

Within the area of your church's minimum factor, it is stimulating to identify the least developed color.

Identifying your color deficiency

Take a look at the diagram to the right. As in previous dia- grams, the bar graph reveals which of the eight quality char- acteristics is your church's present minimum factor. In the case of our example, it is gift-based ministry.

However, this diagram goes one step further. It takes a closer look at the quality characteristic gift-based ministry and indi- cates the color balance in that area. In chapter 3 (pages 106- 121) we saw that each of the eight quality characteristics con- tains three dimensions that correspond to the colors green, red, and blue. For loving relationships, for example, these are the dimensions justice (green), truth (red), and grace (blue). For holistic small groups, they are heads (green), hands (red), and hearts (blue). For gift-based ministry, they are wisdom (green), commitment (red), and power (blue).

A practical example

More on the web:

On the internet (see page 162) you will find answers to the fol- lowing questions:

• Can a primarily "green" believer be a content member of a primarily "blue" church, and vice versa?

• How can the three-color bal- ance be addressed for the qual- ity characteristics that do not yet have NCD tools (with the respective tests) available?

Let's assume that your church has identified gift-based ministry as its minimum factor and has started to address that factor at various levels: leadership, Sunday School, small groups, individ- ual counseling. For assistance in this process, you have decided to use the book, *The 3 Colors of Ministry,* which offers tools to discover both the gifts of the members and their individual starting points with regard to the dimensions of wisdom, com- mitment, and power. Some members may be strong in the com- mitment area, but weak in wisdom and power. Others might display a contrasting starting point: strong in commitment and power, but weak in wisdom. You will probably identify all of the imaginable starting points among the people of your church.

It is helpful for the individual church members to get this information, because it will enable them to focus on the area that is crucial for their personal growth process. If you have a church of 100 people and 70% of them are actively involved in the process, you will have 70 different results showing 70 different color mixes.

As every quality characteristic has a green, red, and blue dimension, it is revealing to identify how balanced these colors are in the area of a church's minimum factor. This picture illustrates these dynamics in the area of gift-based ministry, where the three colors stand for wisdom (green), commitment (red), and power (blue).

A corporate evaluation

Now you can move on to the next question: How does this color mix manifest itself in the whole church? The implementation tools for *The 3 Colors of Ministry* include a CD-ROM with a small program that can easily determine your corporate color mix. Using this tool, you might come up with a result similar to the pie chart at the top of this page: The whole church shows a clear strength in the wisdom area (green); commitment (red) is considerably weaker; and power (blue) is clearly the "minimum color" of your church. Why is it helpful to have this kind of information?

- Such a diagram shows you at first sight the *effects of your church's teaching* about gift-based ministry. In other words, it reveals how balanced your teaching has been in the past.

- It shows you *which area you should focus on* in your attempts to increase the quality of gift-based ministry. In our example, it would be the power area; in other cases, a stronger focus on wisdom or commitment might be the crucial points.

- It helps you select the *most fitting implementation steps*. If your church is strong in wisdom, it is likely to be receptive to teaching and empirical tools such as a test. That may not be the case if blue is the strongest color segment and green the weakest one. In that case, you may need to opt for a more experiential mode of implementation.

Do you know what the color mix of your church's minimum factor looks like?

Chapter 4

Minimum factors of denominations

Recently, the president of a denomination told me, "Twenty-eight percent of our churches are actively involved in the NCD process. Since most of them do their surveys through our denominational headquarters, a great side-effect is that we always have precise and current information about the quality of our churches. Serving as the denomination's president, this kind of information has become invaluable for me. I know exactly where we are as a church body. More importantly, I can observe developments and trends."

> Every denomination should have reliable information about the quality development of its congregations.

How a denominational profile works

While speaking to me, he showed me his most current denominational profile, highlighting the greatest strength, the minimum factor, and the comparison to the situation two years ago. In my opinion, this kind of denominational evaluation best highlights the benefits of the survey.

To obtain a denominational profile, it is necessary that a certain number of local churches have done the survey, and that the results are centrally evaluated. A participation of 30% of the local churches is usually high enough to make observations about the denomination as a whole. Of course, the greater the number of churches involved, the more precise the picture will be.

Examples of four denominations

In our institute, we constantly calculate denominational profiles in order to learn how to minister better to different branches within the body of Christ worldwide. On the

*Profile of **Episcopal** Churches. While all other values are relatively balanced, the two clear minimum factors are passionate spirituality and need-oriented evangelism.*

*Profile of the **Salvation Army**. Their greatest strength is need-oriented evangelism; minimum factors are effective structures and holistic small groups.*

bottom of these pages, I have provided examples of the worldwide results of four very different denominations: Episcopals, Salvation Army, Vineyard, and Assemblies of God.

Please note that these examples, even if they represent thousands of churches from all six continents, are not necessarily representative of these denominations as a whole, but just of those churches that have been involved with NCD. My goal in presenting these diagrams is not to evaluate these denominations, but just to *illustrate* how a denominational profile might look. Since the majority of church leaders are not yet familiar with this kind of health check, it is important that we have seen such a profile in order to appreciate its relevance.

The practical benefits

What are the benefits of having a denominational profile?

- It reveals how strongly developed the *overall quality* of the churches in your denomination is. Some denominations rank considerably higher than others. The reasons for this can always be identified and addressed.

- It helps you set *priorities* and choose themes for denominational activities such as synods, retreats, training events, etc.

- Most importantly, if you regularly profile your denomination, you can easily monitor the *progress* you are making as a whole. It is valuable the other way around as well: If you detect early enough that the overall quality is decreasing, you can take adequate measures to address this situation.

What, would you guess, are the strengths and weaknesses of your denomination?

Profile of **Vineyard** Churches. Their greatest strengths are loving relationships and holistic small groups; their minimum factor, gift-based ministry (albeit at a remarkably high level).

Profile of the **Assemblies of God**. While the other values are relatively balanced without showing a clear minimum factor, their strengths are passionate spirituality and need-oriented evangelism.

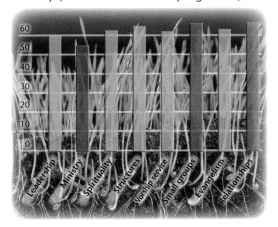

Chapter 4

Minimum factors of whole cultures

In our institute, we have the great opportunity to calculate profiles for entire countries and continents. This is a wonderful way to learn about different cultural identities. While there are many stereotypes of the alleged strengths and weaknesses of various cultures, addressing this question from a purely empirical point of view adds an important dimension.

Focusing on the minimum factor of a country can influence the overall spiritual climate.

My experiences:

Exploring the corporate minimum factor of a country helps me immensely in the preparation of national NCD conferences. It is eye-opening to look at different cultures from the perspective of their corporate strengths and weaknesses. When we developed corporate profiles for the three cultural zones that we have distinguished in the first chapter (pages 28-32), the results were the following: The strength of the West is empowering leadership; the minimum factor, passionate spirituality. In the East, the strength is need-oriented evangelism; the minimum factor, empowering leadership. In the South, the strength is passionate spirituality; the minimum factor, loving relationships.

Confirmed stereotypes and surprises

Sometimes our results have been in line with what could have been expected. For me, it was no surprise at all to discover that...

- the minimum factor of Germany is passionate spirituality;
- the minimum factor of Russia is empowering leadership;
- the maximum factor of China is holistic small groups;
- the maximum factor of the U.S. is inspiring worship service.

In other cases, however, the results came as a surprise. I wouldn't have expected, for instance, that...

- the minimum factor of the U.S. is effective structures;
- the maximum factor of Malaysia is effective structures;
- the maximum factor of Brazil is empowering leadership;
- the maximum factor of Australia is loving relationships.

These "surprises" help us to correct widespread stereotypes about countries. But even in those cases where the stereotypes have been confirmed, we have to remember that the statements concerning the strengths and weaknesses of a given country do *not* apply to the majority of local churches within that country. For example, even if passionate spirituality is the corporate minimum factor of Germany, the majority of German churches have other minimum factors than that. And quite a few German churches show high scores in passionate spirituality.

Without these additional considerations, evaluating countries as a whole could easily communicate almost racist connotations: "Because you are a German, you must be weak in spirituality." For this reason we must be careful how we use national results.

A national process

However, there is an application of the national perspective that isn't driven by curiosity, but by a strategic motivation. In some countries there have been serious attempts to launch a national NCD process. The initial results that we studied as fruit of these "joint ventures" are extremely encouraging. I am convinced that, in the future, we will hear much more about these national processes.

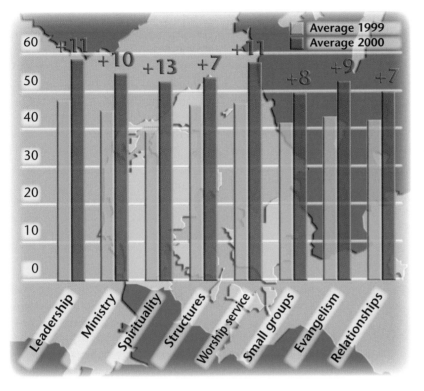

Results of the Danish NCD process: The diagram shows the averages of all profiles that had been conducted at the beginning of the process (yellow bars) and about 20 months later (red bars). Over this time period, the participating churches experienced an average quality increase of 9.5 points.

The diagram above displays the results of a two-year NCD process in Denmark. Almost all of the protestant denominations of the country appointed official representatives to participate in this process. These leaders met twice a year with the goal of being trained as NCD Consultants within their denominations. The really significant things took place between these meetings when the consultants applied their newly gained knowledge to the churches they were responsible for.

Measurable quality increase

At the beginning of the process, all of the churches that were involved in the consultation did the NCD Survey. The results are portrayed by the yellow bars of the diagram. At the end of the process (i.e. about 20 months later), a follow-up survey was conducted. Not every individual church experienced progress, but the average qualitative growth of all participating churches was 9.5 points, which was quite encouraging.

As I was involved in this process myself, along with my colleague Christoph Schalk, I can tell you that in those two years nothing really spectacular happened. We met, had coffee, discussed things, prayed together, set goals, laughed, shared about our experiences, learned from each other, had more coffee. However, the measurable outcome of this unspectacular process was quite spectacular, indeed.

Are there leaders in your country that would be interested in a national NCD process?

Why I like to disappoint expectations

I magine a local church whose greatest strength is passionate spirituality and whose greatest weakness is effective structures. What would be better received, a message on the secrets of prayer or on organizational skills?

Imagine a denomination that is extremely strong in the green color zone with a priority of striving for social justice, but whose red and blue colors are poorly developed. What would be better received, a message on racial equality or on the power of the Holy Spirit?

Imagine a country that has its greatest strength in need-oriented evangelism, while its corporate deficit is empowering leadership. What would be better received, a message on how to win the world for Christ or on how to share leadership responsibility with others?

Overcoming old paradigms

In all three cases, the answers are clear. People applaud you if you minister to them in the area of their strength. They will tell you how anointed your message was, profound and prophetic, inspired and inspiring. If you address the area of their weakness, however, you cannot expect immediate applause. They might tell you that your message created problems, not recognizing that you were only highlighting existing problems. They might tell you that you are a false prophet, not remembering that the majority of biblical prophets swam against the current. They might tell you that they shouldn't have listened to someone from another "camp" anyway—not realizing that this was exactly what they needed to learn.

The themes that are most popular are seldom the themes that are most needed. What people expect of you will seldom be most helpful to them. Because of that, it is a great trap to strive to fulfill existing expectations. Most of the expectations that people have stem from the old and questionable paradigms. If it is our goal to overcome these paradigms (pages 39-40), we cannot fulfill the very expectations that are none other than expressions of these paradigms.

The danger of applause

In my own ministry I have experienced how dangerous it can be to strive for the applause of people. Especially when you have a wide spectrum of topics available—and the trinitarian paradigm offers you an incredibly wide spectrum—it is tempting to choose the very topics that a given group is most receptive to. Such a message would not be unbiblical; on the contrary, it would be in full harmony with the Bible. And yet it would not fulfill what the

---

People applaud you when you minister to them in the area of their strength.

My experiences:

Before I do a conference or seminar, I usually ask the organizers what the group most likely expects of the event. Many organizers misunderstand the motive behind that question. They expect me to fulfill the expectations that they lay out for me. But I ask the question for a different reason. I invest a lot of energy in getting to know the expectations of a group so that I can think about creative ways to disappoint them. I am convinced that striving for the applause of a group by offering them what they expect is one of the chief reasons why so many churches are so imbalanced.

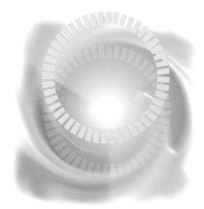

A green starting point

A red starting point

A blue starting point

A blue/red starting point

These diagrams show four differ-ent starting points (solid yellow circles), as they compare to the goal of the journey (transpar-ent circles in the center). In order to move the circle more toward the center, it is neces-sary to stress the opposite colors of the starting point. Since most Christians are still unfamiliar with this kind of approach, initiating such a process often disappoints existing expectations.

Bible expects. It would, willingly or unwillingly, contribute to even more imbalance in the body of Christ. That sort of "biblical message" might result in increasing the very problems it was supposed to solve.

The real impact of the minimum factor approach

This whole chapter has been about the spiritual and strategic signifi-cance of the minimum factor approach. In the past, a number of people have misunderstood this approach as a mere management technique targeted on focusing our energies. Without a doubt, the minimum factor helps you focus your energies. However, my goal in this chapter was to show you that there is more behind it than just that.

The minimum factor approach is the logical consequence of striving for spiritual balance. The attempt to apply a maximum factor approach to all areas of life undermines the goal of spiritual balance. But without bal-ance, there is no health. And without health, we cannot expect growth. In other words, if we want to experience growth, we have no choice but to face that which we are most tempted to flee.

Toward which color area does your church have to move in order to find more balance?

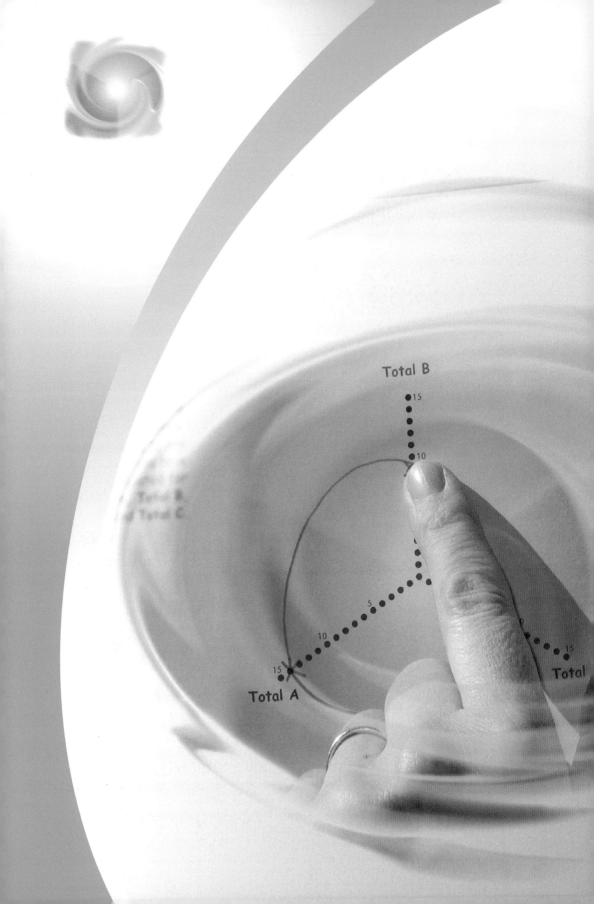

The Tools

5

In Natural Church Development, the focus is clearly on the "internal tools" that you use in order to grow, such as your spiritual gifts, your capacity to build relationships, and your ability to share the gospel. These are the tools that God has already implanted in your life. The problem is that many of us don't know how to discover and release this God-given potential. That is why the Institute for Natural Church Development has developed a number of "external tools" to assist you in this process. There are two hallmarks that all of the NCD tools share: They are built upon the "all by itself" principle and centered around the Trinitarian Compass.

"Do we really need these tools?"

When people ask whether it is necessary to use the NCD tools in order to apply the principles of Natural Church Development, there is only one possible answer: No, it isn't. There are actually NCD enthusiasts who would answer this question differently. They have learned to appreciate the NCD tools and connect them so closely to the principles that they confuse these two categories.

> The purpose of NCD's external tools is to release your internal potential.

My experiences:

In the past, we have been criticized for losing our objectivity when we began to offer practical tools, rather than limiting ourselves to research. Behind this criticism is the hidden assumption that the exclusion of application questions is the best guarantee for objectivity. However, we don't want to be among those scientists who do "pure" research, supposedly uncontaminated by any purpose. On the contrary, our research is expressly designed against the backdrop of practical application.

The function of NCD tools

Jesus never recommended an NCD Survey, but he consistently challenged us to look for fruit. The Bible doesn't speak about the *3 Colors of Love,* but it clearly expects us to grow in each of the areas that the three colors symbolize. Paul never used a *Three-Color Gift-Test,* but he consistently taught and applied the principle of gift-based ministry. Certainly, all of the tools we provide have been designed to help you put into practice these and other biblical insights. But we must never confuse the tools with the principles themselves.

Over the next few pages, I want to introduce you to the major NCD tools we have developed and will continue to develop. You will learn the purpose for which each of these tools has been designed and how you can most profitably take advantage of them. If you don't like them, please don't use them. However, if you decide not to use them, don't stop asking the question of how you can better (more quickly, more sustainably, more cost-effectively) implement the respective principles. And please, let us know about how you have achieved that goal, as thousands of other churches could benefit from your experience.

External and internal tools

Throughout this book, I have repeatedly made a distinction between internal and external tools. The diagram on page 149 illustrates how these two dimensions relate to each other. Even if the realization that *you are a tool yourself* is a key to understanding NCD, having reached this point does not make the use of external tools obsolete. On the contrary, just as any real artist will invest more into the best external tools available than a beginner would, so should the best-prepared churches.

Let's assume you are a great violinist. Your real strength is definitely not your violin (external tool), but your ability to play the violin (internal tool). If this internal tool weren't well developed, you could play a *Stradivari,* but it wouldn't necessarily make beautiful music. However, even if your internal ability to play the violin were strongly developed, you would still need external tools. I could not take you into an empty

You discover a tool

You use a tool

You are a tool

As we saw in chapter one (pages 41-43), there are three phases of development. In the first phase (green segment), you discover a tool. In the second phase (red segment), you learn how to use this tool. In the third phase (blue segment), you become a tool yourself. At this point, you enter the cycle again and learn how to utilize the external tools in new ways.

room, without an instrument, and expect you to show me how great a violinist you are. No, you would need an external tool—a real, physical violin—to demonstrate your internal capacity. And on a *Stradivari* you would perform remarkably better than on an amateur model.

What makes a great cook?

The same applies to a cook. While the amateurs among us might prefer to work without many external tools and just throw a frozen pizza into the oven, anyone who loves to cook and enjoys sharing this art with others, usually has a large number of external tools available: various knives and utensils for unique purposes, a pepper mill, different pots and pans, sources of heat and water. Of course, owning all of these tools doesn't make you a great cook. However, if you are a great cook, I cannot lead you into an empty room and say, "Show me how great a cook you are." You need external tools, and the more developed your internal skills are, the more you will appreciate the quality of the external tools.

It's the same with Natural Church Development. The tools cannot be substituted for your internal abilities, but they can be helpful for developing and utilizing them.

Have you already used "external" tools for church development? If so, which ones?

The basic NCD books

The basic NCD books focus primarily on information, not so much on application and transformation (see pages 41-43). At NCD International, it is our policy that any information on the principles we have identified should be accessible to anyone who is interested in it. It is not our desire to hold back key insights for the exclusive use of selected experts.

The basic NCD books focus primarily on the information level.

The major function of the basic NCD books is to share the insights we have gained with as many people as possible. Let me briefly introduce you to these basic books:

Color Your World with Natural Church Development

The book that you are holding in your hands has been designed to communicate the basic principles of NCD to a wide audience. As it covers both the personal and the corporate dimensions (your own life and your church), it has a stronger focus on the application and transformation levels than the other basic books.

It is beneficial for every church member not only to know these principles, but also to learn how to apply them consistently to his or her life and sphere of influence.

What is an NCD tool, and what is not?

Over the past few years, a number of different tools have been developed that, to varying degrees, are based on NCD principles. In order not to get confused, it is helpful to distinguish the following four categories:

1. Tools developed by NCD International: All of these are consistently based on our institute's worldwide research, strive exclusively to communicate universal principles, and are developed, from the very outset, as international masters for use in different languages and cultures.

2. Additional tools developed by NCD National Partners: Many of the NCD Partners have published additional tools, in most cases as contextualizations for specific needs within their countries.

3. Tools inspired by NCD: Countless other groups have developed their own tools which have been influenced by NCD to one degree or another. Some of them make explicit reference to NCD, some do not.

4. Doctoral dissertations: Over the past few years, Natural Church Development has become a sort of favorite theme for doctoral dissertations in countless universities and seminaries around the globe. Even if some of these might not have much relevance for the actual NCD ministry (you don't usually write an academic work to change the world, or to minister to people, but to earn an academic degree), you will find excellent publications in this category.

Natural Church Development

Natural Church Development is the original introduction to NCD that was published in 11 languages in 1996. Since then, it has been translated into many more languages. This book was designed primarily for pastors, and presents, in contrast to *Color Your World with Natural Church Development,* many observations gained through the original research project. In order to get involved with NCD, you need one of these two introductory books, either *Natural Church Development* or *Color Your World with Natural Church Development.*

Each of these books covers the same principles, but from different perspectives and with different purposes: The first one is to inform church leaders about the research project results; the second one, to get as many people as possible involved in the actual NCD process.

Paradigm Shift in the Church

Paradigm Shift in the Church has been written primarily for pastors and theologians and has become the major NCD textbook in many seminaries and universities. It relates Natural Church Development to the classic themes of systematic theology. Anyone who is interested in studying the theological background of NCD in greater depth may find *Paradigm Shift in the Church* a helpful tool.

The ABC's of Natural Church Development

Finally, I have written a small booklet—a 20-minute read—that offers a quick introduction to NCD. The focus is on the eight quality characteristics. If you have read *Color Your World with Natural Church Development,* you won't find anything new in this booklet. Its main function is to offer a first impression of what NCD is all about. As it is very brief and inexpensive, it can serve as a give-away to larger groups of people. However, the information it provides is not sufficient to help people move into the NCD paradigm.

While the basic book, "Natural Church Development," has been published in many language editions and adaptations, "Paradigm Shift in the Church" is only available in English, German, Korean, Spanish, and Portuguese.

Have you read one of the books mentioned? Are there elements you have already implemented?

Chapter 5

The NCD Survey

In the chapter on the minimum factor I gave you some information on how you could use the NCD Survey as an instrument for constant quality control (pages 132-134). In the next three pages, I would like to explain what kind of information the survey actually provides and how you can most beneficially use it.

Before we make an important decision, we need the best diagnosis available.

My experiences:

It may be important to stress that NCD International has extremely high standards concerning the anonymity of data. While we constantly use the data from the NCD Surveys for our ongoing research, we never communicate any information about individual churches to anybody. We may publish evaluations on the levels of countries, continents, devotional styles, theological orientations, etc., but we would never publish anything in reference to an identifiable local church. While a number of local church profiles have been presented in this book for illustration purposes, I have deliberately refrained from providing any information about the identity of these churches apart from the name of their country of origin. I consistently apply this same principle in my conferences as well.

The scientific formula

If you want to take the NCD Survey, contact the NCD Partner in your country (see page 191). Please note that it is not possible to use the survey of another country or of another language. When the profile of your church is evaluated, the software converts the raw scores of your questionnaires to the numbers shown on the profile. This calculation is based on a standardization formula which is different for every language within a given country.

For example, the Canadian formula for English-speaking churches is different from the U.S. and Australian formulas, and Korean churches within the United States have a different formula than the Korean churches in Korea. You can only expect reliable results when the correct formula has been used. Since churches base far-reaching decisions on the survey results, it is of utmost ethical importance to provide the most accurate information possible. In many cases, the survey literally deals with questions of life-and-death relevance. Providing a wrong diagnosis would have the same serious consequences that it would have in medicine.

The basic profile

After 30 church members have filled in the survey, your church gets the results in the form of a bar graph similar to the one presented on page 153 (central picture). This diagram clearly indicates how strongly each of the eight quality characteristics is developed, specifically revealing your present minimum factor. The price of the survey is set by the NCD National Partners for each country and may differ considerably from country to country. See page 191 for pricing as of the printing of this book.

Constant updates of the system

One of our tasks at NCD International is to provide regular updates of the NCD Survey. While the original survey was based on the results of 1000 churches, the most recent version is based on the results of more than 40,000 churches worldwide. Due to our constantly increasing data base, the quality of the survey increases almost "all by itself." Toward the end of 2006, we will provide a new generation of the survey in an

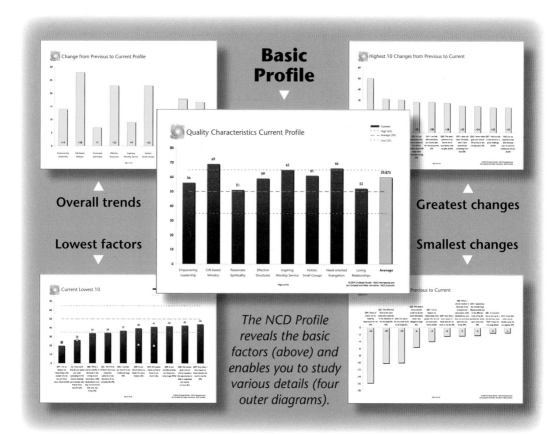

The NCD Profile reveals the basic factors (above) and enables you to study various details (four outer diagrams).

electronic format. There will also be a new version of the *Implementation Guide to Natural Church Development*, but in contrast to the original (printed) edition the new one will be integrated into the electronic format of the survey. The new profile will be modular in nature: While it provides the "basic profile" just as previous versions did, it will enable you to access different modules for background analyses at the same time.

Various modules of background analyses

The picture above shows examples of a background analysis. While you find the basic profile in the center, the new survey will provide a number of additional perspectives (the four outer pictures). For example, it will tell you which items of the questionnaire reveal the greatest (or least) change compared to the preceding survey; it will enable you to access sub-categories and the answers to individual questions; it will help you analyze overall trends, and many other items. Most of these observations are the result of comparing your previous church surveys with one another.

More on the web:

On the internet (see page 162) you will find answers to the following questions:

- *Which modules of interpretation does the most current NCD Survey supply?*

- *Where can I get exact information on the cost of the NCD Survey in my country?*

Please note that you don't have to study all of this background information in order to use the survey; it is absolutely possible to work with the basic profile just as 40,000 churches have done in the past. However, there might be situations in which insights from this background information would be helpful. The modular system will allow you to select just the kind of information you need, without overwhelming you with a several-hundred page report. The basic information will conveniently fit on two pages.

The NCD Survey reveals important spiritual trends.

Misusing the data

As helpful as the information provided by a background analysis can be, some people misunderstand this information. They believe that the more they focus on a detail, the closer they get to the truth. In NCD, however, the opposite holds true. The details—such as the individual items of the questionnaire—are less important than the overall qualities that these items point to.

Let's assume you have identified loving relationships as your minimum factor. In order to evaluate the quality in that area, the survey actually asks many different questions, such as, how often you have invited people for coffee, how much laughter there is in the church, and many more. However, we could have selected different questions to assess the quality of loving relationships. The individual questions that we did select are not the *root factors* that constitute the quality "loving relationships." Rather, they are *indicators* of that quality—symptoms that help us measure how strongly the respective qualities are developed.

Confusing symptoms with root factors

A number of people actually treat the individual items of the questionnaire not as indicators of the quality they hint at (in this case, love), but as individual components that, if put together ("laughter" plus "coffee drinking" plus...) make up the essence of loving relationships. Rather than seeing "love" as the root factor that impacts our behavior in hundreds of areas (those we have addressed on the questionnaire and those we haven't), they treat the individual questions of the survey as the root factors. In the end, they are consumed with how to increase the level of laughter and coffee consumption in the church, rather than creatively asking: How can we remove barriers in our church, so that we can express more genuine love in our relationships?

Have you ever filled out a questionnaire for the NCD Survey?

As in all areas of life, the possibility of misuse should not stop us from providing tools that, if properly used, can tremendously help us get a more precise picture of the situation in our churches. A background analysis can reveal spiritual trends that would otherwise be extremely difficult to detect.

NCD Discipleship Resources

We are in the process of developing one basic book for each of the eight quality characteristics with the goal of helping as many believers as possible live out what the respective quality characteristic is all about. We call this series the *NCD Discipleship Resources*. The books in this series are *not* designed for showing leaders how to implement the individual quality characteristics in their churches. Rather, they address the individual church members, enabling them to increase the quality of their churches by increasing the quality of their heads, hands, and hearts.

However, each of these books is accompanied by implementation tools that address pastors, small group leaders, and mentors. These tools give suggestions for implementing the quality characteristic at the level of the whole church, within a small group, and in a personal discipleship relationship.

The three main criteria

While at first sight the development of these tools might not seem extraordinary, it has turned out to be a mammoth project. This is due to the fact that, in each book, we strive to fulfill the following three criteria:

1. Each of the books is developed from the very outset as an **international master**, designed for multi-cultural usage. Before the first line has been written, great amounts of time have been invested asking the question of international applicability, which includes applicability within different theological traditions and denominations. Since we are interested in teaching universal principles, we usually have to invest a lot of energy in research and field-testing before a specific book can be written.

2. All of the books consistently apply the six **growth forces** without speaking about them. Usually, you won't find any of the growth forces mentioned in the books. When you study the books, however, you will easily detect that the application of these principles is part of the conceptual background. The key behind "all by itself" growth is not to constantly speak about it, but to make its application part of your daily life-style.

3. All of these books place the **Trinitarian Compass** at the center by relating the three-color paradigm to the individual quality characteristic. In order to help the readers identify their starting points, each of the books contains at least one scientifically developed test. For each language version, there is an individual normation of the test to provide accurate results.

All of the Discipleship Resources are developed to be used by a variety of cultures simultaneously.

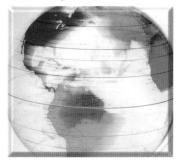

My experiences:

Since the majority of the international versions of the NCD books are translated from English, I decided to write the masters of my books in English. As this is not my native tongue, I am dependent on the help of others. For years, my friends, Jon and Kathy Haley, have invested a lot of energy to help me achieve this task. Throughout the years of our cooperation, I have been repeatedly reminded of the blessing it is to apply a gift-based approach. I am empowered to minister in an area where I have clear limitations, because there are others investing their gifts.

Each of the books applies the three-color approach.

My experiences:

When writing a book according to our international co-production scheme, the first thing I develop is a layout master with different layers for the individual language versions. This constantly reminds me, throughout the process, to focus on international applicability. In the second step I design all of the graphics and illustrations and place them into the layout master. The third step is to simultaneously develop the key terminology for the main languages. All of these steps are finished before the first line of the new book has been written. This is a result of the fact that my mind thinks in pictures and application layers rather than in words. Later on, I add the words to the individual layers to explain the images. In the end, actual writing represents less than five percent of the entire process.

There are many tools available that address—directly or indirectly—the themes of the eight quality characteristics. Many of them are excellent and can be utilized within the NCD process. However, the three criteria mentioned above seem to be unique to the *NCD Discipleship Resources*. We are investing so much energy in the development of these tools, because to my knowledge, no other tools have been developed that fulfill the three criteria mentioned.

The inter-cultural paradigm

The inter-cultural approach behind these tools needs a little explanation, as it is easily misunderstood. Developing international versions of the tools as described above does *not* mean providing versions that are fully contextualized to the specific needs of a given culture. In NCD International, we don't develop tools that are contextualized to the specific cultural or denominational needs of Korea, nor of the United States, China, Indonesia, or Germany. But we strive to provide, for all of these cultures and many more, international tools in various languages that offer enough stimuli for an inter-cultural learning experience.

Why don't we offer fully contextualized versions for each individual culture? Basically, for three reasons:

1. With the exception of two or three cultures, we would simply be unable to do that.

2. As much as this kind of contextualized versions are needed, what they usually do not offer are the challenging stimuli nurtured in a multi-cultural context. Usually, these aspects are "contextualized away," since they are sensed as somewhat strange. In our tools, we deliberately want to offer these "strange" elements to the different cultures.

3. There is absolutely no need for *us* to provide those contextualized versions, as this is the task of the Christians within each individual country.

Contextualized versions

Over the past few years, many of the NCD Partners have developed their own tools, usually to address specific needs in their own cultures. As a result, there are fully Americanized NCD tools available, just as there are native Korean, Filipino, and Danish tools, etc. There is a great need for this category of tools, and I hope that in the future we will see many more of them in all of the major languages on this planet.

Our task at NCD International is to encourage the development of these tools, not to develop them ourselves. Rather, we strive to include in the tools that we provide insights that

At the time of this writing (2005), two of the eight books have already been published: "The 3 Colors of Ministry" and "The 3 Colors of Love." There will be a new release about every two years.

can be learned from different cultural poles, as outlined on pages 28-32. With the NCD tools, we don't intend to provide a "universal theology," but a theological paradigm in which the beneficial co-existence and co-operation of different cultures and denominations can flourish.

I have experienced that in the tool mix that we need, our international versions play an important role. Without materials of that kind, each culture would be in danger of focusing so much on what it is already accustomed to or strong in, that it would completely miss out on what it needs most, which is actually provided by other cultures (see page 32).

Not just for minimum factors

When should each of the *NCD Discipleship Resources* be used? It goes without saying that these books can be beneficial in addressing your church's current minimum factor. However, since it is the constant challenge of any church to maintain and improve the quality in all eight areas, all of the *NCD Discipleship Resources* can be used at any time, and different tools can be used by different groups and individuals in the church simultaneously. In order to check which of the books might be helpful for your purpose, you can download free sample chapters from the NCD web site (see page 162).

More on the web:

On the internet (see page 162) you will find answers to the following questions:

- *How can I discover if a new NCD tool has been released?*

- *What can I do if I am in a language area in which NCD tools are not yet available?*

Have you worked with one of the Discipleship Resources already?

NCD National Partners

Chapter 5

Y ou may or may not be aware of it, but without an NCD National Partner there would be no NCD ministry in your country. Since the work of the National Partners is usually a background activity, many people who are actively involved with the NCD process don't even know that a National Partner exists.

A coach builds a bridge between the NCD principles and the concrete situation of a local church.

My experiences:

Selecting the right National Partner in a given country is quite a challenging task. In some countries we have large and established organizations serving as National Partners. In others, a movement like the Evangelical Alliance has taken over this responsibility. In still others, church leaders have started an interdenominational network with the exclusive purpose of serving as NCD National Partner. And there are other countries where the National Partnership has to be secret, for obvious reasons.

As a matter of principle, we only have one organization serving as the National Partner for each language group in a given country. However, it is not the task of this organization to do all of the ministry on its own. Rather its job is to recruit, train, and support as many sub-partners as possible, usually in different denominations.

The tasks of National Partners

The main tasks of an NCD National Partner are the following:

• Before an NCD ministry can start in a given country, they have to develop a national norm for the NCD Survey, based on a sufficient number of sample churches, in cooperation with NCD International. This is the major reason why, without a National Partner, it is not possible to do the NCD Survey.

• They provide the basic NCD tools and either publish them themselves, or look for a publishing partner within their country.

• They recruit NCD Consultants and support them in their ministry.

• They offer regular conferences and training events, both for the general public and for existing and future NCD Consultants.

• They make the NCD Survey available to churches within their country, usually through their network of consultants or denominational representatives.

• They encourage the application of the NCD principles in a variety of different denominations.

• They are responsible for communication with NCD International. This means that the communication between NCD International and a given country takes place primarily through the National Partners.

Without National Partners, no NCD ministry

Since each of these tasks is vital for developing an NCD ministry, without an NCD National Partner in a given country there is no NCD ministry. If you should be in a country where no NCD ministry exists and you believe it would be beneficial for your country to have such a ministry, you could look for

At the time of this writing, there are NCD National Partners in about 70 countries. Since the partnership situation is in constant flux, check the most current information on one of the NCD web sites.

a group that shares this vision and is both willing and able to take over the responsibility of being an NCD National Partner.

As a matter of principle, NCD International *never* initiates a National Partnership. We exclusively wait for groups who are interested in this kind of ministry to contact us. Once such an interest has been expressed, we do our very best to help launch a national NCD ministry. NCD National Partners aren't branches of NCD International, but independent organizations. Every single one of them has its own style and support structures.

The benefit of NCD Coaches

Since the majority of NCD Partners have built up a network of coaches who have been trained both in the NCD principles and in coaching techniques, you may want to consider if your church could benefit from the ministry of an NCD Coach. Just as any pastor has to build a bridge between the Word of God and the people, it is the primary job of a coach to build a bridge between the universal principles of NCD and the concrete situation in a local church. In this process, NCD Coaches are advocates of "all by itself" growth. Their job is to help you release the potential that God has already implanted in your church. Whenever NCD Coaches "push" you, you can be sure that they are seeking to push you to focus on the six growth forces. Often the most crucial part of their ministry is nothing other than asking the right questions at the right time.

Different NCD Partners have developed very different coaching systems. Some do the coaching in networks (i.e. pastors of a region meet in support groups that are facilitated by an NCD Coach), others prefer to send coaches directly into local churches; some focus on denominational coaching, others on interdenominational coaching events. As with all of the NCD tools, there is no right or wrong. Look at what is available and choose what best fits your situation and your personal style.

Have you already encountered the ministry of the NCD National Partner in your country?

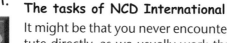

Chapter 5

NCD International

We try to build the ministry of NCD International according to the same principles that we teach to local churches. This includes striving, as consistently as possible, to model a "David" rather than a "Goliath" approach (page 36). In all areas of our ministry, we apply a pure network approach. On page 161, you can see a picture of our fully-functional office in Northern Germany; my colleague, Christoph Schalk, has an additional office in the south of Germany. We have several employees and free-lancers who live in different countries and are connected to us mainly through the internet.

In all areas of ministry, NCD applies a pure network approach.

The tasks of NCD International

It might be that you never encounter the ministry of our institute directly, as we usually work through the NCD National Partners in the various countries. The primary job description of NCD International is to recruit and support those partners. Among other things, this encompasses the following tasks:

NCD International...

My experiences:

At NCD International, we strive to apply the NCD principles to our financial policy. This has meant for us that, from the outset, we have rejected two common financial systems: First, we decided not to build the ministry on outside donations, but tried to establish a self-sustaining financial structure. Second, we decided not to establish a ministry that bases its decisions on commercial considerations. We exclusively finance the work we do from the financial feedback that the ministry itself produces: seminar fees and royalties from NCD tools.

• constantly evaluates the data from the NCD Surveys to better understand the growth dynamics of churches, and publishes the most relevant results;

• helps develop different national adaptations of the NCD Survey;

• selects suitable NCD National Partners in countries where no NCD ministry exists and assists them in developing an NCD ministry;

• develops international versions of NCD tools that are based on research and published in different language editions;

• helps organize the international co-productions for various NCD tools;

• supports the National Partners in offering training events in their countries;

• works on constantly updating and revising all of the NCD tools (such as the NCD Survey and the books);

• is responsible for the ongoing communication with the various NCD Partners and helps them solve problems that emerge in the ministry.

A pure network

By functioning as a pure network, we don't have any sort of legal authority over other groups or individuals. Whenever people put the things we suggest into practice, it is exclusively because it makes sense to them. I believe that this informal structure is one of the major reasons for the quick and sustainable growth of the NCD network. No NCD Partner, no

Headquarters of the Institute for Natural Church Development: a former farm at the Danish/ German border. The house is well-equipped, including electricity, running water, and internet access.

consultant, no bishop, no local church does anything because they have to, but exclusively because they are convinced of its significance.

This is also the reason why we don't work with the endorsements of famous people—a generally accepted practice both in the Christian and non-Christian world. Of course, we know that those endorsements could motivate people to get involved with NCD. However, we don't want them to get involved because a prominent leader suggested it, but exclusively because *they* are convinced it is the right thing. Deliberately and strategically building on this inner conviction rather than on outer authority has given the NCD Community remarkable stability.

Prayer needed

You cannot support NCD International through donations. This is not because we have too much money; on the contrary, due to the initial research projects and a number of unexpected challenges, we still face considerable debts. The reason for rejecting donations is simply that it would be against our principles to finance our ministry in that way. We are convinced that the major problems that Christianity faces in the area of church development are not of a financial kind, but have to do almost exclusively with questionable paradigms in our heads and hearts.

Would you consider adding the ministry of NCD International to your prayer list?

We don't want your money, but we depend on your prayer. If there should be readers who value our ministry and decide to put us on their prayer list, our whole team would thank God for you.

Chapter 5

The NCD Web Sites

There are a number of different web sites that deal with Natural Church Development. Since NCD functions as a network, the internet supplies an ideal platform for communication within the NCD Community. Through the following three sites you can access everything that is important within the NCD world.

The international portal: www.ncdnet.org

This is the central international NCD portal that includes links to everything else. If you don't know exactly what you are looking for, start here. The content provided on this site is primarily geared toward leaders. Here you will find online training and various downloads. You can also subscribe to a free NCD online magazine. This domain contains a password-protected area that is only accessible to NCD National Partners. The site is in English.

The NCD Web Sites connect you to the worldwide NCD Community.

The Three-Color web site: www.ncd-international.org

This site may be interesting for leaders as well; however, the focus is on a wider audience. It places the Trinitarian Compass at the center and provides information on all available NCD tools, including free downloads of sample chapters of the books. It also includes videos introducing the NCD ministries in various countries. The site is in English.

There is a sub-category of this web site (ncd-international. org/community) specifically designed for readers of this book. The main purpose is to provide background information to all of the chapters. By registering with your e-mail address and inserting your access code provided on the yellow bar to the left, you can view this site. It is available in various languages. For example, the mini-seminars on the six chapters of this book (see margin text to the left) are provided for most of the languages in which this book has been published.

Your access code:
CYW-US-378-509-321

Registered readers of this book get free access to the web site www.ncd-international.org/ community. There, among other things, you will find: six mini-seminars that I have put together on each of the six chapters of this book; background information on the contents of every chapter; and the graphics of this book for use in your own presentations. Your access code is provided above.

Domain of your NCD National Partner: see page 191

Many of the NCD National Partners have their own domains that feature various kinds of content. One of their greatest values is that they give you access to additional tools that these partners have developed. Another advantage of these sites (or disadvantage, depending on your perspective) is that they have been designed in the languages of their respective countries.

Check page 191 for the web site of the NCD National Partner in your country. Links to the web sites of all National Partners are provided at www.ncd-international.org.

There are a number of different NCD web sites, most of them geared toward pastors, coaches, and leaders. The web site pictured here has been designed for a wider audience.

Focus on achieving results

The NCD web sites have not been designed to keep you as long as possible on those sites nor to come back as often as possible. On the internet, there are countless commercial sites that have been strategically developed to do just that, and all of us know how annoying it can be when our time is stolen in that way.

To me, following that procedure is another example of confusing "results" with "measures to achieve a result," as we have dealt with on pages 36-38. Many providers of internet content actually measure their "success" by the time that people spend on their sites, rather than what people achieve as a result of the help that is provided therein. The time you spend on an internet site is a classical example of a "measure to achieve a result." If you can achieve your results effectively by visiting a specific site only shortly or seldom, I would define it as a "successful" site. I, for one, would like to see you putting NCD principles into practice, not spending your time surfing the internet.

Constantly updated information

However, it can be beneficial to check the sites mentioned above every now and then, as they are frequently updated. To keep in touch with developments, I recommend you subscribe to the free NCD online magazine, especially if you are interested in special training events or the NCD Campaign (see next two pages).

Could any of the information or tools accessible through the internet be helpful to you?

Chapter 5

The NCD Campaign

A s we have seen throughout this book, the essence of Natural Church Development is not a campaign, but an ongoing process. What is the difference?

An NCD Campaign is a concerted effort to connect members of various churches and cultures.

• A campaign has a clear beginning and end; a process is a long-term commitment.

• A campaign builds momentum; a process goes on even if the momentum decreases.

• A campaign is targeted on immediate results; a process seeks long-term fruit.

• A campaign is a public event; a process is a hidden background activity.

• A campaign is relatively easy to plan; a process has less predictability.

Not either-or, but both-and

In the past few years, we have deliberately focused on presenting NCD as a process and have stressed its long-term character. Without a doubt, we will continue to do this, because it is this long-term orientation that is the key to success. However, we believe that the time has come to offer, along with and in addition to it, a specially designed NCD Campaign to all churches that might be interested. The frustrating thing with many campaigns is not the campaign itself, but that it tends to replace the long-term, less spectacular local church processes.

More on the web:

On the internet (see page 162) you will find answers to the following questions:

• *What is the date of the next international campaign?*

• *Which campaign tools are available?*

Thanks to God's grace, in the NCD Community we now have a different starting point. Thousands of churches around the globe have invested in the NCD process for years and are experiencing encouraging results. We are convinced that an NCD Campaign, performed in addition to this, can considerably speed up the process and attract people that wouldn't have been attracted otherwise.

Features of an NCD Campaign

An NCD Campaign is characterized by the following features:

• It has basically the same ingredients as the process, but everything is presented in a condensed, momentum-building format.

• It is a time-limited, five-week event offering special worship services, small group activities, training sessions, prayer events, etc.

• *Color Your World with Natural Church Development* serves as the text-book of the campaign (see appendix on pages 184-190); apart from that, there are specifically designed campaign tools.

• It is focused on involving 100 percent of the worshipping congregation; everybody is exposed to basic NCD training.

NCD Campaigns are held on all six continents simultaneously. By participating in the campaign, church members can experience firsthand what it means for NCD to be a truly global community.

- It has a "two-track" structure: While the leadership track focuses on the NCD Survey; the member track is focused on the personal and corporate Color Profiles.
- It is simultaneously performed on all six continents with one central event that is broadcast over the internet.
- It is accompanied by research. The question is not how many people have participated in the campaign, but rather, what is the qualitative and quantitative increase one year after the campaign?

A concerted effort

In the past few years, we have repeatedly heard many churches express that this kind of "concerted effort" would be a tremendous help. Sure, it is realistic to assume that not every church involved with the campaign will make a long-term commitment to NCD. However, it can be expected that the number of churches that do make such a commitment will be higher as a result of the campaign than it would be without it.

One of the greatest benefits of the campaign is that it will be simultaneously performed on all six continents. As all of the participating churches will be connected through the internet and special events, not only will the whole NCD family work together in a concerted effort, but it will also *experience* what it means to work together. For that reason, we recommend joining the international campaign schedule. If that schedule doesn't fit the time requirements of your church, it is possible, of course, to do the campaign in a reduced format as a purely local church event. For current information, please visit the NCD web sites (page 162).

Could participation in an NCD Campaign help your church progress?

Your Starting Point

A generic, step-by-step plan for spiritual growth does not exist. People might have to move in different directions—even opposite directions—in order to get closer to the center. For that reason, the steps that you need to take may be extremely different from someone else's. The same holds true for whole churches. However, once you have identified your individual starting point it is usually quite obvious what your next steps ought to be.

Chapter 6

Identify your starting point

The purpose of this chapter is to help you apply the information of the preceding five chapters to your personal life and the life of your church, using the results of your NCD Color Profile (pages 72-79). The goal is to move from information to application, and possibly even begin opening the door to transformation (see pages 41-43).

Before you consider your next steps, you must know where you are.

My experiences:

When writing or speaking about the implementation of NCD, I usually structure my teaching according to different "points." However, I regularly change both the number of points and the contents of each point. Sometimes people are confused by this and ask, "In your book you wrote about ten implementation steps, but now you have only shared six. Which is correct?" The answer is that there is no right or wrong. Implementation steps are not principles. They are only suggestions of how principles can be put into practice. By constantly changing my teaching on this topic, I hope to demonstrate that we should never become dogmatic about a specific method of implementation.

Step 1: Understand the concept of a starting point

I hope that the preceding chapters have helped you catch a vision of where you would like to go, both personally and with your church. If so, you might be interested in having concrete steps for getting there. However, it is still too early to deal with this question. Before deciding which steps you need to take, you not only have to know where you want to go, but also where you presently are. You cannot plan practical implementation steps until you have compared your starting point with your future destination. To clarify this point, let me summarize the three necessary steps:

1. Discover **where you currently are** (the NCD Color Profile and the NCD Survey help you answer this question).

2. Decide **where you would like to go** (this is a personal decision; however, the Trinitarian Compass can serve as a helpful reference).

3. Develop **practical steps** that will help you move from point 1 to point 2 using the NCD principles.

It really doesn't matter whether you contemplate step 1 or step 2 first, but it is important to wait to address step 3 until you have clearly answered points 1 and 2.

Why the sequence matters

Why do I emphasize this sequence? It has been my experience that people who don't have precise answers to the first two points (What is my starting point? and Where do I want to go?), tend to confuse them with each other. They either interpret their present situation in the light of their future expectations, i.e. they see their current reality in a far-too-positive light. Or they project their difficult present situation on the future reality, which is equally counterproductive, as it makes it almost impossible to radically change the situation.

In both cases, points 1 and 2 *are* moving closer together, but they are only moving together on your map, so to speak, not in reality. If your starting point is already so close to your destination or your destination is not that different from your starting point, there is no longer any need for a journey (point 3). That is the reason why it is so essential to have precise answers to points 1 and 2 before considering practical

Throughout this book, you have encountered this picture several times. It helps communicate, at a glance, the concept of a starting point.

steps. This also explains why we, at NCD International, have focused so strongly on developing tools for addressing points 1 and 2. Once these questions have been settled, the answers to point 3 fall into place more easily.

The dynamics of the Trinitarian Compass

Take another look at the picture at the top of this page and recall the dynamics of the Trinitarian Compass that you have encountered throughout this book: Everyone has a different starting point... Where you are weak, others are strong... People might need to move in opposite directions in order to get to the same destination... Your church as a whole may represent a different starting point than you do... Never project your experiences on others... Believers representing different starting points can help each other reach their destination...

Well, before you accuse me of being repetitive, I'm going to assume that you get it. If you are not absolutely sure, it could be helpful to refresh your understanding of the five rules of the Trinitarian Compass (pages 66-68).

Step 2: Accept your personal starting point

Having done the NCD Color Profile, you already have an indication of what your starting point looks like. I don't know your personal results, but there are two things I do know:

1. You have identified one color segment that is more strongly developed.

2. You have identified another color segment that is least developed.

Of course, it is possible that two of the colors show the same scores or even that the whole picture looks relatively balanced. Nevertheless, having read the first five chapters of this book, you will probably be able to indicate certain tendencies concerning your strongest and weakest areas.

Accept where you are, but don't stay there for the rest of your life.

My experiences:

It is my experience that the majority of Christians misunderstand the concept of "accepting" other people's or churches' starting points. "Can you really accept that liberal position?", an evangelical pastor recently asked me after I had shared about working in a denomination that is strongly influenced by syncretism, relativism, and a "God-is-dead" theology. My answer was, "Yes, I accept it— as a starting point. In the same way, I accept legalistic or spiritualizing tendencies—as starting points." Of course, I sometimes wish that churches had different starting points. But what I wish is not what's important. I have to accept reality as it is, if my interest is really in helping churches become healthy, rather than just telling them how wrong they are.

Celebrate your strengths

What are you supposed to do with these results? First and foremost, accept them. Celebrate your strengths, since they are divine gifts. And don't fight against your weakness, but look for creative ways to grow in that area. Remember that everyone has strengths and weaknesses. Paul had them, Peter had them, Moses had them. Only Jesus had a perfectly balanced profile. Since you are not Jesus, you don't need to be upset if your profile is just like mine: out of balance.

Since the next few pages will focus on your least developed color, I want to stress that, before you address your weakness, you should rejoice in your strength. In the past few years I have encountered a number of believers, local churches, and whole cultures that have had an incredibly low self-esteem, even in their areas of strength. Whenever I have detected that, I have postponed the application of the minimum factor approach. Focusing on your minimum factor can be counterproductive, if you are unable to appreciate your strengths. I have seen situations in which an exclusive focus on learning how to appreciate one's strengths was necessary for several months before being able to beneficially apply the minimum factor approach.

Step 3: Accept your church's starting point

One of the most important principles that NCD Coaches are taught is to accept the starting points of the churches they are ministering to, regardless of their own theological or spiritual bent. If they are not able to do this, they cannot serve well as coaches. You probably aren't a coach, therefore applying this principle doesn't imply the need to adapt to constantly changing situations.

You may have the results of your church's Color Profile on hand, or perhaps your church has done the NCD Survey. As a member of your church, you need to apply the same skill that we teach coaches: You must accept these results, whether you like them or not. You would probably love to see changes; however, until you are able to accept the situation as it is, you will be unable to help your church experience change.

The solid yellow circle depicts the typical starting point of a "green" church: strong in green, weak in both red and blue. You cannot help such a church move closer to the center (transparent circle) until you have come to appreciate its strengths.

No preconditions

In NCD International, we are quite dogmatic about the following rule: There are no preconditions for getting involved with NCD. I must confess that there are some NCD enthusiasts who communicate a different idea. In their eagerness to stress the seriousness of the whole undertaking—a concern that I wholeheartedly share—they start to set up preconditions that a church must fulfill, such as: "You can only get involved with NCD if you fully own the principles of NCD, if you are committed to a long-term process, if your church has reached a certain size, if you hire a coach, if you can sign this doctrinal statement, etc."

Without a doubt, it is nice if a church meets some of these preconditions. It makes life easier. However, we should never present as a precondition that which can be anticipated as a result of an NCD process. A church could be thoroughly heretical in its theology and still be invited to enter the NCD process. However, chances are good that in the course of the process its theology will be transformed. By excluding those churches from entering the process, we would also have excluded them from experiencing theological and spiritual change. Never assume that accepting your church's starting point is the same as being content with the situation as it is. Rather, accepting the starting point is a precondition for any sort of change.

Putting the Trinitarian Compass to work

Since I have frequently been invited to speak to groups that represent "questionable" starting points (in all three directions of our trinitarian paradigm), I can tell you that the dynamics of the Trinitarian Compass really work. Recently I dealt with a thoroughly "liberal" denomination where 45 churches had done the NCD Survey. With the exception of only four churches, all of them had identified "passionate spirituality" as their minimum factors.

I showed them the diagram on page 171 and asked them if they could identify with it. "Sure," they said, "that is exactly our situation." We started the process by celebrating their strengths: caring for the poor, fighting for social justice, racial integration. After we had done that, we focused on the color deficiencies of this group, the red and blue zones.

I spoke very little throughout the whole event, largely limiting myself to asking questions, such as, "What are the hindrances to growth in the red and blue zones?" The group put together a list of these hindrances and discussed it. The next question was, "What can we do to overcome these hindrances?" They considered the question in small groups and presented the results. Their list included items such as "prayer nights," "altar calls," "discipleship processes," "revision of theological education," and even "spiritual warfare." I didn't suggest any of these ideas. Those liberal pastors came up with them on their own. When reflecting on this list, you must not forget that hearing a thoroughly liberal pastor speak about "altar calls" comes close to seeing an anti-charismatic walk on water or a puritan transform water into wine!

Moving closer to the center

I have asked exactly the same questions in a number of liberal groups and have experienced the same results every single time. I have tried the same approach in "blue" and "red" churches—the results were the same. How can it be that all of these different groups react so positively to the same message? I believe it is due to the fact that their respective strengths are appreciated and their weaknesses are not addressed from an attitude of criticism or pride: "If you want to be a true Christian, you have to be like me, because I am the perfect representation of a balanced believer." Rather, the message is that we can all learn from each other in order to move closer to the living God.

> ### Accepting one's starting point is a precondition for any sort of change.

More on the web:

On the internet (see page 162) you will find answers to the following questions:

- *Does the dominance of one of the colors indicate an easier starting point than the dominance of another color?*

- *Are there churches in which the Trinitarian Compass doesn't work?*

Describe both your personal and your church's starting points.

Strive for balance in your own life

Let's summarize where you are. If you have decided to read this book on a purely informational level, the answer is easy to give: You are on page 173, and the next page will be 174. However, if you have decided to *apply* the information to your life, the answer is not as straightforward. What I know is that you definitely have done the NCD Color Profile and have identified your present starting point. You have also dealt with the Trinitarian Compass and have an idea in which direction you should move in order to bring more balance to your life.

What I don't know, however, is what you are feeling. Does the prospect of delving into a color area that may be outside your comfort zone evoke feelings of curiosity or feelings of fear in you? Sharing your answers to this question with a group of fellow believers could be of great value to you at this point.

If you are a pastor or hold another leadership position in your church, take a closer look at your own life before getting side-tracked thinking about your church. Please don't read the next few pages with the following question in mind: "How could my people strive for more balance in their lives?" Instead, ask yourself, "How can I become more balanced?" One of the most sustainable contributions that a leader can make is to model the process of personal growth.

Step 1: Acknowledge that every believer is out of balance

We have mentioned this principle already, but now is the time to put it into practice. Since every believer is out of balance, you don't need to feel like you have a life-threatening illness. Rather, consider that you are working with a personal fitness trainer who suggests you focus on a muscle group that you have previously overlooked. If your own imbalance should be more severe, rejoice that it has been brought to your attention. As a result of this diagnosis, you will be able to take the right steps in order to apply a fitting therapy. The result will be restored health—a prospect that really shouldn't be too threatening.

The same thing that applies to you, applies to everyone else. Expect other people to be out of balance. Treat it as the most normal thing in the world. Don't let biographies convince you that the respective hero was a perfectly balanced person of God. Learn to speak openly about your own imbalance and the imbalance of others. Nurture a climate in which it is fun to share about these personal things. It is only shameful to be out of balance when we are not striving to bring more balance to our lives.

Many of us avoid thinking because we are afraid of the consequences.

My experiences:

Years ago, I was part of a committee where hardly anyone thought through their ideas before presenting them. We talked a lot, but we didn't think. Finally, as I had the distinct impression that those meetings were a waste of people's time, I complained. The leader told me, "You are right, Christian, most of us are simply too busy to think." I suggested that next time we start our meeting thirty minutes later in order to give us thirty minutes to think things through at home. It didn't work. It would have been far easier to have gotten together two hours earlier to continue our poorly prepared exposition of ideas. No, most of us are really not too busy to think. We avoid thinking because we are afraid of the consequences. Therefore, we prefer to be busy.

Step 2: Focus on the opposing pole of your current strength

Every strength is related to a specific danger. If your strength is in the reflective area (green), your danger zone is rationalism. If your strength is in the proactive area (red), your danger zone is activism. And if your strength is in the affective area (blue), your danger zone is emotionalism (see page 58). The principle of focusing on the opposing pole of your current strength implies that it is more productive to strengthen the color segment located opposite your strong color (which is also the color of your danger zone) than to fight against your danger zone.

Take some time to reflect on what the application of this principle means for you in practical terms. Regretfully, many people never take time to thoroughly think these things through. They get started, but stop midway. Don't do that. Sometimes it's just a matter of adding ten more minutes to your thought process, before you experience a spiritual breakthrough in your life.

Learn to speak openly about your own imbalance and the imbalance of others.

More on the web:

On the internet (see page 162) you will find answers to the following questions:

• How can I learn from Christians of another color segment if they have a fundamentalist attitude?

• As a leader, is it wise to speak about one's own imbalances?

If the concept of focusing on the opposing pole of your current strength still sounds a bit abstract to you, do the following:

• Take the graphical representation of your Color Profile on page 78.

• Mark an "X" in the area of your greatest strength. If one color clearly dominates, draw the "X" in that area. If two colors are relatively well-developed, while the third one is weaker, make the "X" between the two well-developed colors.

• Now look for the opposing pole. If you have placed your "X" between red and blue, the opposing pole is green. If you have placed your "X" within the red segment, your opposing pole is "green/blue." Indicate the area of your opposing pole with a large "O".

• Consider the terms highlighted in the captions next to the diagrams on pages 61-65. These terms describe what the three colors are meant to communicate. Write down the terms that relate to the opposing pole of your current strength.

• Think about each of these terms. Try to come up with examples of these features in action (both from your own life and the lives of others). Underline the two terms that speak to you most.

• Write down concrete actions that would help you strengthen the features that you have underlined.

• Focus on these points for at least the next two weeks. Observe what happens. If possible, share your discoveries with fellow believers.

If you want to grow in a certain color area, seek the help of those who are already strong in that segment. You may, in turn, help them in their growth process.

Step 3: Network with people whose strength is your weakest color

The previous exercise was something you could do completely on your own, with just this book and a pencil in front of you. You will add power, speed, and fun to your growth process if you go one step further. Look for people whose greatest strength is in the color area of your greatest weakness. It won't be difficult to find these people, if you have done the Color Profile with your small group or your whole church. Share the result of your Color Profile with them. Ask them to share their experiences in the color area of their strength, using the terms provided in the diagram on page 47 and looking for practical examples.

Then, if the other person is open to this, change roles. Since you are strong in the color zone where the other is weak, you can share how the color of your strength has manifested itself in your life. Look for concrete measures that would help the other person grow. I have frequently conducted similar exercises at NCD conferences. My experience has been that it usually takes some time to break the ice, since many of us are not accustomed to this kind of sharing. However, after a while, discussion tends to flow without the need for additional prompting.

Keep in mind that this kind of activity is more than spiritual entertainment. For me, it is symbolic of how the body of Christ should function, even if we don't have color profiles and books in front of us. It is my hope and prayer that these mutual support processes will gradually become part of many churches' normal life-style.

What is the most important thing you can do to bring more balance to your life?

Chapter 6

Invest in a more balanced church

When you proceed to apply the NCD principles to your local church, keep in mind that the preceding steps have already contributed to the health of your church, even if the focus was primarily on yourself. Since the church is nothing other than people, increasing your own spiritual health is a direct contribution to the health of your church.

Increasing your own spiritual health is a direct contribution to the health of your church.

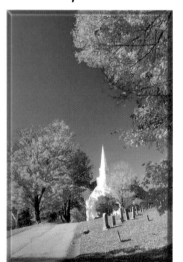

My experiences:

When analyzing the data in our files we discovered that an increasing number of churches involved with the NCD process have decided to give birth to new churches. If you compare all churches that have already planted a daughter church with those that haven't, the quality in the first category is 5 points higher. In addition, the numerical growth rate of a mother church is considerably higher than in churches that are not reproducing.

Let's assume that only 30 percent of your worshipping congregation is involved in the process of improving their own spiritual health by focusing on their weakest color areas. You would clearly detect the results upon conducting another NCD Survey. The measurable quality of the church would be higher.

In reality, the "church" that the survey measures is people; we don't ask the church pews to answer the questions, we ask the people sitting in the pews. And we don't ask them to evaluate the pews, but to speak about the reality in their heads, hands, and hearts.

Step 1: Analyze the results of the NCD Survey

Up to now, we have primarily focused on the NCD Color Profile. If you conduct it at the level of the whole church, it will provide eye-opening results. It will reveal how balanced your church is. This simple information will help the leadership of your church plan activities in such a way that your church reflects "God's fullness." To get your church's results, follow the procedure on page 72.

However, in this section I would like to come back to the NCD Survey that was described in more detail on pages 132 and 152. This tool focuses on the eight quality characteristics of healthy churches and helps a church identify its current minimum factor.

If you repeatedly take the survey, you will be able to detect trends in the qualitative development of your church. The diagram on page 177 gives you an example of two profiles that have been conducted within 18 months of each other. Comparing these two bar graphs reveals a lot about what took place in this church in the 18 months between surveys.

Differing levels of openness

It may be that your church has already taken the NCD Survey numerous times, or that the whole idea is still new to your church leadership. If the second is true, consider which of the three following categories your church represents:

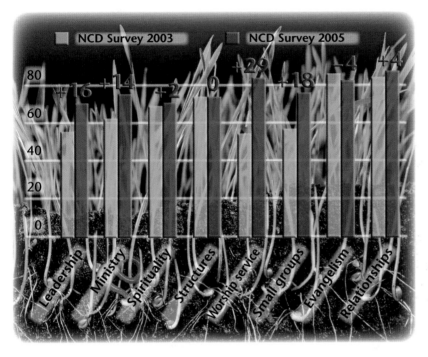

Comparison of two NCD Surveys from a church in the United States: With the exception of two quality characteristics (effective structures and need-oriented evangelism), there had been qualitative increase in every area. The most dramatic growth, however, occurred in the area of the former minimum factor, inspiring worship service.

1. While the idea of taking the survey is still foreign (because it is new), the leadership regards this option with interest and curiosity.

2. Your church is not interested in the NCD Survey, since the leaders apply a "different approach" to church development.

3. The idea of doing the survey is rejected, as the paradigm of the church categorically rules out applying such a procedure.

If the *first* option applies, supply your leadership with the necessary information. Don't focus on the technical aspects, but on the practical benefits.

If the *second* option holds true (i.e. the church is not interested in taking the survey because it is following a "different approach"), clarify what NCD is all about: helping your church become more effective in reaching the very goals that are important to your church. Most likely your church leaders consider Natural Church Development to be "another model." In that case, communicate clearly that NCD is about universal principles that apply to all sorts of churches and church models.

If the *third* option applies (i.e. the survey is rejected because the church's paradigm categorically rules out such a procedure), don't waste your energy trying to convince anyone to do the survey. In this situation, there are far more important things to do than convincing people of the relevance of an empirical study. The very paradigm that doesn't allow for the NCD Survey will have negative consequences on other areas of church life as well, and these consequences are far more serious.

If you are faced with such a situation, consider praying for a crisis, as times of crisis are usually an ideal introductory event. Don't misunderstand me. The NCD Survey has not been designed as a tool for crisis intervention, but as an instrument for continuous quality improvement. However, the occurrence of a crisis can be an ideal time to introduce Natural Church Development. Depending on the nature of the crisis, it may not be wise to start with the NCD Survey, but to suggest other elements of NCD, such as the Trinitarian Compass or simply working on one of the quality characteristics, such as "loving relationships."

> Regularly evaluating the quality of your church is an extremely eye-opening exercise.

My experiences:

When a church experiences crisis, the majority of its people are upset. That is understandable, since incidents that create crises are usually negative incidents. However, from a church development point of view, times of crisis are ideal for introducing a "new" approach, such as NCD. There is hardly anything more frustrating than an unhealthy church that is content with itself—neither growing nor declining, experiencing neither crisis nor revival. Such a church doesn't usually see any reason for change. A crisis, however, highlights this need dramatically. If a crisis occurs, we should thank God!

Step 2: Enter the NCD Cycle

Do you remember the section titled "I have done NCD" (page 17)? That was about churches that have gone as far as described above and have firmly believed they have "applied NCD." It is probably overly clear by now that Natural Church Development should not be reduced to taking the survey, but that it is an ongoing process.

Our Australian NCD Partners have expressed this idea in the form of a cycle (see diagram on page 179). I like this representation very much, as it communicates at a glance that NCD is not a "six-step program," but a process with different "seasons." Each year the church takes a new snapshot of its health and works on the least healthy area. Although the stages of the cycle remain the same, the process is different every year because the minimum factor changes, experience increases, and the church itself changes.

The NCD Cycle is really a two dimensional picture of a health spiral. As you do the Cycle every year, consistently removing barriers to growth, your church progresses up the health spiral. The Cycle stages highlight process steps that ensure sustainable progress: you prepare the church for the survey; you do the survey regularly to assess progress; you analyze the results carefully to identify barriers to growth; you work out a plan to address those barriers; you implement the plan and refine it as change occurs; and you stop and assess progress each year before continuing onto the next phase of growth.

Constantly removing growth barriers

What is the NCD Cycle all about? If you apply it consistently to your church, your main focus will be to constantly identify barriers to "all by itself" growth (these may be emotional, intellectual, spiritual, or institu-

A graphical representation of the NCD Cycle: Natural Church Development is not a "six step program," but an ongoing process. Each year the church takes a snapshot of its health and works on the least healthy area. Although the stages of the cycle remain the same, the process will be different every year because the minimum factor changes, experience increases, and the church itself changes.

tional barriers) and to set specific qualitative goals for overcoming each of these barriers. Finally, you will monitor the degree to which you have reached your goals.

Note that taking the NCD Survey is an integral part of the cycle, assuming that this is done once a year. Why once a year? Because only when we integrate the survey into a regular cycle, can we expect to make it a normal, undisputed, firmly established background activity. The goal of the cyclical format is to develop a certain regularity and routine. For many churches, the idea of taking the NCD Survey is still far too big a hurdle, associated with controversial discussions, exaggerated hopes, and unjustified fears.

For this reason, I like to compare taking the survey with counting the offering. You probably don't ask after every worship service: Should we count the money or not? Is it really spiritual to count it? Isn't it God's sovereign task to count the money? Wouldn't it be better to trust our intuition rather than add up the figures? Isn't it premature to count it now? Shouldn't we wait three more months so that we can expect better numbers? Is our church really prepared to deal with the fact that giving has decreased? Will people become unspiritually proud if they hear that this week the offering was 10% higher than last week?

Whenever I use this analogy, people tell me that counting money is different to measuring the quality of a church. Of course, I know that. But honestly, what kind of information is more relevant for church leaders, information concerning the offerings or concerning the qualitative development of the church? I don't want to answer this question for you, but if I were a leader of a local church, I would have no doubt which kind of information is more important.

Step 3: Monitor your progress

The diagram on page 181 illustrates the results of four surveys that a church took over four years. At first sight, the diagram might look confusing. Don't forget, however, that it represents quite complex dynamics: the qualitative development in eight different areas within four years. Throughout this process, there had been times of crisis and celebration, times of focusing on the NCD process and being busy with other challenges. Whatever the church did during these four years has left visible marks on the diagram.

Time and again, people tell me that it is not really spiritual to do these kinds of surveys. Interestingly enough, they are the same people who have no spiritual qualms with counting the offerings every week, bill by bill and coin by coin, adding up the results in a long, boring list. Let's assume you had similar data to what is represented in the diagram on page 181, for your own church. Wouldn't it be highly relevant—spiritually relevant—to carefully analyze these developments? Again, I leave the answer to you.

The movement is the decisive factor

When interpreting this kind of data, the most important point is not the static information reflecting where you are at the moment. The most important point is not the scores that you got. The most important point is not even the minimum factor that the profile currently displays. Rather, the most important point is the *development* between different profiles, as this is a representation of the actual *movement* that your church has taken.

When studying the diagram on page 181, you will see that in most areas there have been ups and downs, but it is instantly visible that the church is moving in the right direction.

Constantly identify barriers to qualitative growth and set goals to overcome them.

My experiences:

The "worst" church profile that I have ever seen came from a church in Iowa. While in most churches the scores rank between 35 and 65, the results of their first profile was –2 (minus two). Their minimum factor, empowering leadership, was –22. Anyone, with or without training in NCD, could tell that this church had a problem. However, after ten months of work, they took a second profile and their new average score was +33. That was still far below average. It was still not a healthy church. It still couldn't expect to grow, and it shouldn't even consider multiplying. Yet, the qualitative growth from –2 to +33 is a dramatic case study of what "success" in NCD means: not reaching a static point of excellence, but being involved in an ongoing growth process.

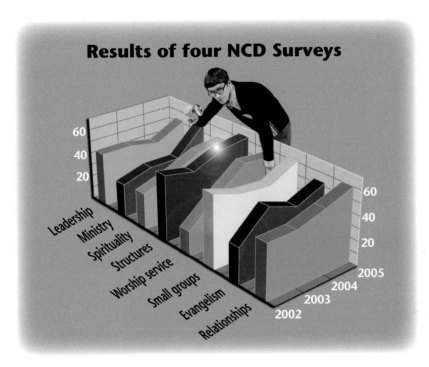

Results of four NCD Surveys

Leadership
Ministry
Spirituality
Structures
Worship service
Small groups
Evangelism
Relationships

2002 2003 2004 2005

Comparison of four NCD Surveys taken from a church in Germany. In most areas, there were ups and downs over the years, but the overall tendency was a steady increase in quality. Without such a graphical representation, it would be extremely difficult to speak about qualitative development in precise terms.

Expect a breakthrough

You might remember that in the first chapter (page 20) I wrote about a "breakthrough pattern," and my primary evaluation was critical. In using this term, I was referring to people who are so focused on spiritual breakthrough that they fail to recognize the very things that tend to cause a breakthrough.

Let's apply this notion to our potted plant analogy (page 128), and define "breakthrough" as the plant's production of enormous amounts of fruit. When is that most likely to happen? When we consistently apply the principles of natural growth, or when we ignore them? When we bring all of the essential factors (nutrients, water, location, size of the pot) into balance, or when we focus on a "water-only" approach? The answer is self-evident.

Consistently applying the principles portrayed in this book, striving for spiritual balance, and growing in quality, will give you more reason to expect a breakthrough. This breakthrough could manifest itself in many more people being attracted to your church, a new experience of spiritual power, an increasing impact on society, or just an overwhelming feeling of joy deep down in your heart.

More on the web:

On the internet (see page 162) you will find answers to the following questions:

- *When we do a repeated survey, should it be the same, or different, people who fill in the questionnaire?*

- *Where can I get more information on the NCD Cycle?*

Where is your church in the NCD Cycle, and how can it move to the next stage?

Chapter 6

Your next step

Communicating by means of a book is a rather strange undertaking. I have to write a message that applies to all different starting points imaginable, to liberals and fundamentalists, to pastors and lay people, to members of megachurches and of house churches, to congregations that have already achieved a high level of health and those that are struggling with serious illness, to those who have applied NCD for years and to those for whom all of this is brand new.

Take a moment to reflect—and then take a courageous next step.

My experiences:

I recently spoke about the principles shared in this book at an NCD conference: the Trinitarian Compass, the eight quality characteristics, the six growth forces, the minimum factor approach. At the end of the conference, a journalist approached me for an interview. I sensed that he didn't really feel comfortable at that conference. He had the impression that the topics were so esoteric and inner-church related that they didn't have any impact on the concern he was interested in: how to change society. Almost ironically, he asked me, "Do you really believe that with your NCD activities, you will change the world?" My answer was brief: "Yes, I do."

Your personal starting point

To a certain degree, I believe that the Trinitarian Compass has helped me tackle this communication problem, as it enables me to address very different starting points with the very same words. But I deliberately said, "to a certain degree." If I were sitting next to you now, we would definitely be having a different form of communication than we are having now.

At the end of a book that has focused so much on long-term processes, I would love to suggest one concrete step that you can take. However, from what I have written, you will understand that I am not able to offer you this step, and you probably wouldn't feel taken very seriously if I told you now, here from my office in Emmelsbüll, Germany, what you have to do as a next step. You have to discover that on your own. However, in the light of your personal Color Profile and that of your church, I trust that an answer to this question will not be too difficult to find.

What you can expect

I don't know the situation of your church, but what I do know from our research is that churches that are involved with NCD and have done three or more surveys, have increased their quality by 6 points and their growth rate by 51% within only 31 months (see page 12). In other words, to expect such results is not extraordinary, but absolutely realistic. Take a moment to think through where you could be in 31 months if you were to make the right decisions and take the right steps right now.

This book has spoken about growth and decline, about crisis and revival, about persecution and expansion. The fact is that for countless churches, none of these categories applies. There is neither growth nor decline, neither crisis nor revival, neither persecution nor expansion. There is just stagnation. Nonmovement. Standstill. Both in quality and quantity, every year it is exactly the same picture. People don't really hate these churches. They simply find them boring and irrelevant.

I am not worried about churches that are declining or that have low quality. Those things can be changed. Thirty-one months from now they could find themselves in a completely different situation. However, if there is no movement at all, if no one sees the need to change anything, if there is not even an awareness that this standstill *is* the strongest form of crisis—that sort of situation is something that frightens me. Since I have seen with my own eyes what can be achieved in no more than 31 months, since I have seen churches with the worst imaginable starting points make remarkable progress, since I have seen revivals taking place in the midst of the NCD Community, I am not willing to accept an absolute standstill.

There are no "bad" starting points. The only hopeless situation is one that you are unwilling to address.

A holy impatience

Don't misunderstand me. When I am dealing with a church that suffers from its present situation and would like to see change, but has to face a lot of difficulties and only makes extremely slow progress, I am usually patient, tolerant, and understanding. However, when dealing with a church of the kind described earlier—one that is not aware of any problems whatsoever—I immediately get impatient, intolerant, and demanding, and I believe that this shift in my behavior is spiritually prompted.

If you are facing a situation of that kind, I want to explicitly encourage you to become impatient, intolerant, and demanding as well, in the name of the Triune God. Don't accept such a situation. Tell the leaders that there *are* alternatives, and that it is their responsibility to take the right measures to initiate change. The facts are available. The principles of church health are not secret knowledge. We can know what we need to know if we want to know.

If the thousands of Christians who are members in these churches would display this sort of holy impatience, wouldn't it make a difference? It would. It's definitely not pleasant to be around impatient, intolerant, and demanding people. But in such a hopeless situation, our task cannot be to be "pleasant" people. Many of us have played this role for decades already. It hasn't been overwhelmingly successful. It's time to try a different approach.

More on the web:

On the internet (see page 162) you will find answers to the following questions:

- *What could be my personal "next step" if my home church is not open to NCD?*

- *What could be my personal "next step" if my church has never heard about NCD?*

God has called you

On the other hand, if you are a member of a church that is striving to grow in quality and quantity and supports you in your attempts to become a more balanced believer, thank God for it. Thank God for your pastor. Thank God for your whole church leadership. Pray for them every day. Don't get frustrated if you encounter problems. Don't get impatient with people who are slow at learning. Don't get angry with those who fear change. All of that is normal. Thank God for choosing you to be what you are: An essential part of his plan to reveal his love to millions of people.

In light of what you have read, what is the most important step you should take at this moment?

Appendix

Suggestions for studying this book within an NCD Campaign

As explained on pages 164-165, this book has been designed to be utilized within church-wide NCD Campaigns. These campaigns are simultaneously performed in various countries on all continents, so that the participants will experience first-hand the spiritual benefits of the inter-cultural approach that is at the heart of NCD.

Please note that churches that register for the campaign usually get large discounts on the book. Apart from that, they get access to a web site from which they can download specially developed campaign tools.

If you are interested in participating with your church in such a campaign, please visit *www.ncd-international.org/campaign*.

Campaign motto:
Color Your World with God's Love

Throughout the campaign, all participating church members will study the book, *Color Your World with Natural Church Development,* on a daily basis. The goal of this process is to integrate all three levels of learning—information, application, and transformation (see pages 41-43). In their weekly small groups, the participants will discuss their personal experiences. The worship services will focus on each week's theme:

Week 1: Learning from the whole family of God

We were all baptized by one Spirit into one body—whether Jews or Greeks, slave or free—and we were all given the one Spirit to drink. Now the body is not made up of one part but of many. —1 Cor. 12:13-14

Week 2: Reflecting all of God's love

We, who with unveiled faces all reflect the Lord's glory, are being transformed into his likeness with ever-increasing glory. —2 Cor. 3:18

Week 3: Experiencing "all by itself" growth

I planted the seed, Apollos watered it, but God made it grow. —1 Cor. 3:6

Week 4: Enhancing the health of our church

The whole body, joined and held together by every supporting ligament, grows and builds itself up in love, as each part does its work. —Eph. 4:16

Week 5: Taking practical steps

We are God's fellow workers; you are God's field, God's building. —1 Cor. 3:9

In the campaign, the focus is not so much on Natural Church Development, but on coloring your world with *God's love*. In this process, *Color Your World with Natural Church Development* functions as a tool designed to fulfill this purpose.

Week 1

Appendix

Theme of the week:
Learning from the whole family of God
(Chapter 1)
The first week highlights the practical benefits of being part of a global family of believers with different cultural and denominational identities. It demonstrates what it means in practical terms for Christians of different backgrounds to strive to learn from each other.

Day 1
Your dream church • Startling results from 70 countries (pages 10-13)

> *To him who is able to do immeasurably more than all we ask or imagine, according to his power that is at work within us, to him be glory in the church. —Eph. 3:20-21*

Day 2
The NCD Story • "I have done NCD" (pages 14-18)

> *I will build my church, and the gates of Hades will not overcome it. —Mt. 16:18*

Day 3
What is your favorite growth pattern? (pages 19-22)

> *Everyone who hears these words of mine and puts them into practice is like a wise man who built his house on the rock. The rain came down, the streams rose, and the winds blew and beat against that house; yet it did not fall, because it had its foundation on the rock.—Mt. 7:24-25*

Day 4
Natural Church Development and spiritual unity • The qualitative approach—often criticized, seldom understood (pages 23-27)

> *Make every effort to keep the unity of the Spirit through the bond of peace. —Eph. 4:3*

Day 5
Why we need to learn from other cultures (pages 28-32)

> *All over the world this gospel is bearing fruit and growing, just as it has been doing among you. —Col. 1:6*

Day 6
NCD in an age of hype • Who is your hero: David or Goliath? (pages 33-38)

> *Whoever finds his life will lose it, and whoever loses his life for my sake will find it. —Mt. 10:39*

Day 7
Why all of us need to check our "spiritual glasses" • Information, application, transformation—what's needed most? (pages 39-43)

> *Do not conform any longer to the pattern of this world, but be transformed by the renewing of your mind. —Rom. 12:2*

Week 2

Theme of the week:
Reflecting all of God's love
(Chapter 2)

The second week focuses on the central role of spiritual balance. There-fore, the Trinitarian Compass is placed at the center. The participants will relate the dynamics of the Trinitarian Compass to their own lives and receive the results of their own Color Profile, both on a personal and corporate level.

Day 1

My personal "trinitarian pilgrimage" • The center of theology (pages 46-48)

> *Love the Lord your God with all your heart and with all your soul and with all your mind. —Mt. 22:37*

Day 2

You can reflect God's light • How God communicates with you (pages 49-53)

> *God is light; in him there is no darkness at all. —1 John 1:5*

Day 3

Let's strive for spiritual balance • The New Jerusalem—descending to earth • Why Christianity is in such a bad state (pages 54-59)

> *He measured the city with the rod and found it to be 12,000 stadia in length, and as wide and high as it is long. —Rev. 21:16*

Day 4

What you can learn from green churches • What you can learn from red churches • What you can learn from blue churches (pages 60-65)

> *Test everything, and hold on to the good. Avoid every kind of evil. —1 Thess. 5:21-22*

Day 5

Five rules of the Trinitarian Compass (pages 66-68)

> *I will not boast about myself, except about my weaknesses. —2 Cor. 12:5*

Day 6

The Trinitarian Compass and the doctrine of the Trinity (pages 69-71)

> *There are different kinds of gifts, but the same Spirit. There are different kinds of service, but the same Lord. There are different kinds of working, but the same God. —1 Cor. 12:4-6*

Day 7

The NCD Color Profile • Your spiritual roadmap (pages 72-79)

> *You are the light of the world. A city on a hill cannot be hidden. —Mt. 5:14*

Week 3

Appendix

Theme of the week:
Experiencing "all by itself" growth
(first part of Chapter 3)
The third week lets the participants experience what "all by itself" growth is all about. While the first day presents the concept of "all by itself" growth in context, each of the following days deals with one of the six growth forces. These days are not so much focused on intellectual information, but rather on considering how each of these principles can manifest itself in our own lives.

Day 1
Principles—the inflation of a term • Understanding "all by itself" growth • Two different sets of principles • Six growth forces (pages 82-91)
> *A man scatters seed on the ground. Night and day, whether he sleeps or gets up, the seed sprouts and grows, though he does not know how. All by itself the soil produces grain. —Mk. 4:26-28*

Day 2
Growth force 1: Interdependence (pages 92-93)
> *The heavens declare the glory of God; the skies proclaim the work of his hands. Day after day they pour forth speech; night after night they display knowledge. —Ps. 19:1-2*

Day 3
Growth force 2: Multiplication (pages 94-95)
> *The things you have heard me say in the presence of many witnesses entrust to reliable men who will also be qualified to teach others. —2 Tim. 2:2*

Day 4
Growth force 3: Energy transformation (pages 96-97)
> *We know that in all things God works for the good of those who love him. —Rom. 8:28*

Day 5
Growth force 4: Sustainability (pages 98-99)
> *Unless a kernel of wheat falls to the ground and dies, it remains only a single seed, but if it dies, it produces many seeds. —John 12:24*

Day 6
Growth force 5: Symbiosis (pages 100-101)
> *The entire law is summed up in a single command: Love your neighbor as yourself. —Gal. 5:14*

Day 7
Growth force 6: Fruitfulness (pages 102-103)
> *Every good tree bears good fruit, but a bad tree bears bad fruit. —Mt. 7:17*

Appendix

Week 4

Theme of the week:
Enhancing the health of our church
(second part of Chapter 3 and first part of Chapter 4)
The fourth week deals with the eight quality characteristics and the minimum factor approach. When considering each of the eight areas, the focus is still on the Trinitarian Compass and its application to our personal lives. At the same time, the whole church body is addressed. If your church has done the NCD Survey, this week would be an ideal time to communicate the results to the whole church.

Day 1
Eight quality characteristics • Quality characteristic 1: Empowering leadership • Quality characteristic 2: Gift-based ministry (pages 104-109)
> *Each one should use whatever gift he has received to serve others, faithfully administering God's grace in its various forms. —1 Peter 4:10*

Day 2
Quality characteristic 3: Passionate spirituality • Quality characteristic 4: Effective structures (pages 110-113)
> *The Sabbath was made for man, not man for the Sabbath. —Mk. 2:27*

Day 3
Quality characteristic 5: Inspiring worship service • Quality characteristic 6: Holistic small groups (pages 114-117)
> *Where two or three come together in my name, there am I with them. —Mt. 18:20*

Day 4
Quality characteristic 7: Need-oriented evangelism • Quality characteristic 8: Loving relationships (pages 118-121)
> *God has poured out his love into our hearts by the Holy Spirit, whom he has given us. —Rom. 5:5*

Day 5
How to apply these principles • Where the minimum factor applies—and where it doesn't (pages 122-127)
> *Now it is required that those who have been given a trust must prove faithful. —1 Cor. 4:2*

Day 6
Learning from a potted plant • The image of the minimum barrel (pages 128-131)
> *See how the lilies of the field grow. —Mt. 6:28*

Day 7
Application 1: Quality characteristics • Application 2: Trinitarian Compass (pages 132-137)
> *Examine yourselves to see whether you are in the faith; test yourselves. Do you not realize that Christ Jesus is in you? —2 Cor. 13:5*

Week 5

Theme of the week:
Taking practical steps
(Chapter 6 and some pages of Chapters 4 and 5)
While the preceding four weeks incorporated practical application, the fifth week deals exclusively with practical steps. The goal is not to provide new information, but rather to relate the information gathered within the process to concrete decisions and commitments.

Day 1
Identify your starting point (pages 168-172)
> *Do not think of yourself more highly than you ought, but rather think of yourself with sober judgment. —Rom. 12:3*

Day 2
Strive for balance in your own life (pages 173-175)
> *If you think you are standing firm, be careful that you don't fall. —1 Cor. 10:12*

Day 3
Invest in a more balanced church (176-181)
> *Let us make every effort to do what leads to peace and to mutual edification. —Rom. 14:19*

Day 4
The broader picture: The texts for this day—all from chapter 4—show what can be expected if the NCD principles are applied to whole churches, denominations, countries, and continents (pages 138-145).
> *Go into all the world and preach the good news to all creation. —Mk. 16:15*

Day 5
The tools at your disposal: On this day, the participants scan through chapter 5, which introduces the various NCD tools. The goal is to see if there is anything that might help them achieve the goals they have set in the previous stages. There is no need to study this chapter to the same extent as the previous ones (pages 146-165).
> *Offer yourselves to God, as those who have been brought from death to life; and offer the parts of your body to him as instruments of righteousness. —Rom. 6:13*

Day 6
Your next step (pages 182-183)
> *I do not consider myself yet to have taken hold of it. But one thing I do: Forgetting what is behind and straining toward what is ahead. —Phil. 3:13*

The results of NCD

If you are considering participating in an NCD Campaign (see page 164), it may be helpful to review the results of NCD to date: Churches that have done three profiles, have seen the following measurable changes within the 31 month between the first and third profiles:

- The **quality** of the church (in all areas of church life) increased by an average score of 6 points.

  Translated into practical terms this means: deeper prayer, livelier small groups, more loving relationships, more energizing worship, more satisfied commitment, greater engagement with one's culture, greater attractiveness among the unchurched, etc.

- The **growth rate** increased by 51% on average.

  As a direct consequence of the NCD process, 1.3 million additional people have joined the participating churches. That is significant since the process itself isn't characterized by an evangelistic focus, i.e. the additional growth was exclusively a natural side effect of focusing on church health.

- The percentage of "transfer growth" (people joining from other churches) decreased while the percentage of **conversion growth** increased.

  At the outset, churches participating in the NCD process have the same starting point as any other church: If they are already experiencing growth, the percentage of transfer growth is usually too high and the percentage of conversion growth is too low. Within the NCD process, this ratio changes quickly in favor of conversion growth.

- The **work load** of the participating members decreased significantly.

  Of the 170 items tested, this is the result with the second strongest change. The positive response to the statement, "Despite my church activities, I have sufficient time for my hobbies" grew by 9.3% within the 31 months between the first and the third profiles. This corresponds to a measurably higher level of satisfaction in the church among those who are personally involved in it.

The five-week campaign *Color Your World with God's Love...*

- offers churches that want to get involved with NCD a condensed introduction to the process;

- energizes those churches that have already been involved with NCD and generates momentum that draws in those members that haven't yet been a part of the process;

- can serve as a "trial run" for those churches who are not yet sure whether or not to get involved with a long-term process.

More information at:

www.ncd-international.org/campaign

How to conduct the NCD Survey

Appendix

I f your church is interested in the NCD Survey, it can be purchased through ChurchSmart Resources. As of the printing of this book, the survey is sold at $150 (price is subject to change). This includes 30 surveys for key lay people and one for the pastor. The cost also includes the scoring, the *Implementation Guide to Natural Church Development,* the *Minimum Factor Manual,* and discussion questions related to your minimum factor.

If you have questions or would like to place an order, please feel free to contact us at:

ChurchSmart Resources
3830 Ohio Ave.
St. Charles IL 60174
U.S.A.

Phone: (800) 253-4276
E-mail: orders@churchsmart.com

Information on all of our products and training events is also available on our website at:

www.ChurchSmart.com